Books should be returned on or before the
last date stamped below.

BELIEVE IT OR NOT!

David J. Randall

Published by Rutherford House

First published 2000
by Rutherford House, 17 Claremont Park,
Edinburgh EH6 7PJ, Scotland

06 05 04 03 02 01 00   7 6 5 4 3 2 1

British Library Cataloguing in Publication Data

A catalogue record for this book is available from
the British Library

ISBN 0-946068-82-8

Ba

1312376

Typeset by Rutherford House, Edinburgh
and Printed by
T.J. International Ltd., Padstow, Cornwall

CONTENTS

Chapter 1

A Real Footstep in the Hall?

You possibly know John; he may be a member of your family, a neighbour, a friend or someone you know at work. He is a decent and cheery person who is happily married and has a grown-up family. He was brought up to believe in God, and in his younger days it seemed to John that good citizenship, belief in God and decent living all went together. Today, however, he has a changed attitude. You would hardly ever see John in the church he joined as a teenager. Looking back now, he sees his attitude at that time as naive and idealistic. Many things in life have seemed to him to put up barriers to that whole attitude of faith which he once accepted more or less uncritically.

The truth is – he really doesn't feel any need for what religion claims to offer. Through hard work, he and his wife have achieved a high standard of comfort; their home is tastefully furnished, they can afford good holidays, and they feel that they have earned what they enjoy. They are quite content with their secular attitude and lifestyle.

John would tell you that he doesn't have anything against religion; in fact, when the local parish minister calls, they have a good-going debate on religious issues. But there are so many things that would make it hard to believe nowadays.

He could list them for you. He has seen so many dreadful things happen in his lifetime that he says he can't any longer believe in a God of love. He feels that science and technology have taken the place which 'God' once occupied in people's thinking. 'And,' he would ask, 'in a pluralistic world like this, how can Christianity claim to be the only way to God?' If you were to ask John about the church, he would tell you about many church members he has known who have not lived out the precepts of Christianity, he would refer to terrible things which have been done in the name of Christianity, and he would tell you that, when he did go to church, he found it dull and boring. He would agree with the view that, if people have spiritual needs, they should seek their own answers wherever their own spirits may lead them.

This book is written for people like John. We hope it will encourage him to take another look, to reconsider whether his secular outlook is a valid one, and to think again about the issues which he has come to see as barriers to Christian faith.

To believe or not to believe...

That is the question.

The actual barriers identified in our opening paragraphs about John were all mentioned in a survey conducted under the auspices of the Church of Scotland in 1993. Elders and others were encouraged to find out 'on the ground' what issues constitute barriers to belief in the minds of our contemporaries.

Martin Robinson of the Bible Society has written:

All too often Christians assume that they know what concerns non-Christians have, without really making much attempt to research that area. In reality, very little research – if any – has been undertaken into what concerns occupy the minds of the unchurched.[1]

Well, the Church of Scotland's survey represented one attempt to find out what the real issues are.

The last chapter of this book gives more information about this 'Barriers to Belief' survey; if readers wish to find out more about the background to this book and the selection of subjects with which it deals, they might like to read that last chapter first. Otherwise, let's get right into it!

The book has been written amid the demands of ongoing pastoral ministry, and it is hoped that this means that it is related to 'real life' and to 'real people' (people like John) rather than being an academic or theoretical exercise in apologetics. Apologetics it hopefully is, but not in a way that is detached from real life. It seeks to take account of the very real issues which keep people from believing today.

It is also set within the context of seeking after what is true and right. In the last chapter, we will consider the Bible's assertion that 'the things that come from the Spirit of God... are spiritually discerned' (1 Cor. 2:14); it is the Holy Spirit's illumination that creates the spark of spiritual life. But, as Augustine said long ago, the fact that it is God who gives the increase does not mean that we need not plant and water. Alan Richardson quotes these words in the context of saying, 'The gift of sight is always a miracle of divine grace; but this does not mean that Christians may sit still and take no trouble to make ready the way of the Lord.'[2] Our hope is that 'John' will reflect afresh on the claims of Christianity, with an open mind and a willingness to be led wherever the evidence may take us.

The following chapters deal with many issues which are said to be barriers in the way of faith (see next section), but there is one other which was not in fact mentioned by people who responded to the survey. One might wonder whether, however strong the arguments might be, some people would not be convinced because they do not wish to be convinced, or because they are not prepared to face the demands which might be involved in Christian commitment. We would not wish to imply that there is no such thing as honest doubt, or that all unbelievers share such an attitude – of course not. But at the same time, it is surely true that sometimes people are held back more by an unwillingness to face the demands of Christ than by the kind of barriers mentioned in this book. The question is sometimes posed as to why, if Christianity is true, the majority of intelligent people do not believe it. Could it be, at least sometimes, for the same reason that the majority of unintelligent people do not believe it – namely, that they are unwilling to face the demands which such a commitment would involve?

Our hope is that 'John' will be prepared to follow wherever the evidence may lead in this fresh look at the alleged barriers to belief.

Four types of barriers

The people who were asked if they could identify what were the barriers to faith in their own minds made mention of many issues, and in the report, *Understanding The Times*, which was presented to the 1995 General Assembly of the

Church of Scotland, these barriers were categorised and presented under four headings:

1) Barriers which relate to what might be called 'intellectual' issues, such as suffering, science and pluralism (not 'intellectual' in any rarefied sense, because such issues are often intensely practical also). We will look at these in chapters 2, 3 and 4.

2) Barriers which relate to the secular climate of our times. These will be taken up in chapters 5, 6 and 7.

3) Barriers which relate to the life of the church itself, which is seen by many to be a barrier to belief. In chapters 8 and 9 we will consider what people say about the church's past record and its present image.

4) Barriers which stem from the lack of any felt need of what Christianity claims to offer. These will be dealt with in chapters 10 and 11.

A footstep in the hall

In 'Miracles', C. S. Lewis was discussing differing concepts of 'religion': 'An 'impersonal God' – well and good. A subjective God of beauty, truth and goodness, inside our own heads – better still. A formless life-force surging through us, a vast power which we can tap – best of all.'

But then he goes on: 'But God Himself, alive, pulling at the other end of the cord, perhaps approaching at an infinite speed, the hunter, king, husband – that is quite another matter.'

And then he brings in a homely illustration:

> There comes a moment when the children who have been playing at burglars hush suddenly: was that a *real* footstep in the hall? There comes a moment when people who have been dabbling in religion ('Man's search for God'!) suddenly draw back. Supposing we really found Him. We never meant it to come to *that!* Worse still, supposing He had found us?[3]

Clearly, Lewis did not mean that the approach of God is to be seen as frightening or threatening. In the last chapter we will consider Christianity's claim that it is the very opposite of that. But Lewis graphically draws attention to the possibility of someone realising that it's not just make-believe; maybe that was a *real* footstep in the hall. Could there really be Someone there?

Notes

1. M. Robinson, *A World Apart* (Monarch Publications, Tunbridge Wells, 1992), p.178.
2. A. Richardson, *Christian Apologetics* (SCM, London, 1947), p.28.
3. C. S. Lewis, *Miracles* (Collins, London & Glasgow, 1947), p.98.

Chapter 2

Why Doesn't Life Work?

The reality of suffering is one of the factors which presents a barrier to belief for many people. This is no new thing, but it is a very real thing, perhaps underlined by the immediacy of modern reporting through television, with people's tragedies being brought into our homes on a daily basis. People ask, 'How can we believe in God when there is so much suffering and evil in the world?' And, apart from knowing about others' troubles, so many people have felt what Lloyd George felt when a doctor brought him the news that his daughter had died. He simply said, 'Why doesn't life work?'[1] He had been discussing political, economic and national issues when the news was brought to him, but suddenly all such issues took a back seat as he was brought up against the kind of personal and practical difficulties which confront most of us sooner or later.

The same thing was expressed very forcefully and succinctly by a nurse whose statement contains only ten words, but says a great deal: 'No-one who has nursed cancer patients can believe in God.'[2] That, of course, was not the comment of someone sitting in an ivory tower trying to build a philosophy; it was the comment of a practical person trying to cope with the realities of life, and we can feel the passion in her statement.

Once I visited a man who was dying of cancer. He had lived a good life, taken an active part in Church work and sought to honour God in his life. Now, however, he was in considerable distress, and as I left him, knowing that I would not see him again in this life, I couldn't help thinking, 'Lord, if we have to die, why couldn't it be easier than this?'

This great 'Why' question is one which is found in the Bible. For example, Psalm 10 begins with the word 'Why?'. It is interesting that it is *to God* that the Psalmist addresses the question, yet he asks, not with cool detachment but with passionate heat: 'Why, O Lord, do you stand far off? Why do you hide yourself in times of trouble?' That's how it seemed to him. He had been tested. He had seen the dreadful and wicked things some people do, and seem to get away with. The following verses go on to describe 'the arrogance of the wicked man (who) hunts down the weak.... He boasts of the cravings of his heart; he blesses the greedy and reviles the Lord', and, so far as any notion of regard for God is concerned, 'In his pride the wicked does not seek him; in all his thoughts there is no room for God.'

Similarly, the book of Habakkuk begins with a great complaint against God, which is striking for its contemporary sound:

How long, O Lord, must I call for help, but you do not listen? Or cry out to you, 'Violence!' but you do not save? Why do you make me look at injustice? Why do you tolerate wrong? Destruction and violence are before me; there is strife, and conflict abounds. Therefore the law is paralysed, and justice never prevails. The wicked hem in the righteous, so that justice is perverted (Hab. 1: 2-4).

If it were to be suggested, as the prophets frequently taught, that God was working out his purposes even through wicked people and wicked actions, Habakkuk would protest:

Your eyes are too pure to look on evil; you cannot tolerate wrong. Why then do you tolerate the treacherous? Why are you silent while the wicked swallow up those more righteous than themselves? (Hab. 1:13)

Again, Psalm 22 gives expression to the feeling of God-forsakenness. It begins with the desperate cry, 'My God, my God, why have you forsaken me? Why are you so far from saving me, so far from the words of my groaning?' The Psalmist writes about crying out to God day and night, and yet there seemed to be no answer. His belief that God had helped his forefathers made his plight all the worse, as also did the fact that cynics taunted him with things like, 'He trusts in the Lord; let the Lord rescue him.' Actually, this Psalm is quoted more in the New Testament than any other, and it is interpreted in particular in relation to the sufferings of Jesus on the cross, but for the moment, we simply hear its anguished cry as another instance of the Bible's own recognition of the reality of this problem.

Hebrews 4:15 says about Jesus, 'We do not have a high priest who is unable to sympathise with our weaknesses'; the same could be said of the Bible. It is not incapable of understanding our troubles and problems; it is not too heavenly-minded to be of any earthly use. Hebrews goes on to the exhortation, 'Let us then approach the throne of grace with confidence, so that we may receive mercy and find grace to help us in our time of need', but before we ask what Christianity can say on this issue, let us reflect further on the reality of the problem.

A real problem

The 'problem' is particularly acute for people who have some kind of belief in God.

It is that belief in the existence of an almighty and loving God that raises the issue and makes us ask the question, 'Why?'. Putting the matter the other way round, the question might be posed: if you do not believe that there is a God, why should you expect everything to be happy and blissful? If we human beings are just chance products of an impersonal universe, and there is no rhyme or reason to anything that happens, why should we count the existence of suffering and evil to be a 'problem'? (That is, in the philosophical or theoretical sense; obviously we all have the same practical problems in coping with bad things that happen.)

A poem by Steve Turner[3] gives forceful and provocative expression to this point about the consequences of unbelief:

If chance be
the Father of all flesh,
disaster is his rainbow in the sky,
and when you hear 'State of emergency!'
'Sniper kills Ten!'
'Troops on Rampage!'
'Youths go Looting!'
'Bomb blasts School!' –

It is but the sound of man
worshipping his maker.

However, for those who believe, or want to believe, in God, there is a problem. It is *made* a problem by three things which many would practically take for granted.

1) The first is the reality of suffering and pain. We cannot sensibly dismiss such things as imaginary or illusory.

Aldous Huxley makes short shrift of the notion that pain is illusory in this exchange between two characters from *Brave New World*:

'Pain's a delusion'.
'Oh, is it?' said the Savage and, picking up a thick hazel switch, strode forward.
The man... made a dash for his helicopter.[4]

And there is the well-known limerick:

There was a faith-healer from Deale,
Who said, 'Although pain is not real,
When I sit on a pin
And it punctures my skin,
I dislike what I fancy I feel.

2) The second factor which contributes to the problem is the Christian teaching that God is almighty. If there is a God at all, then presumably by definition he is almighty ('omni-potent'), and if that is so, it means that he *could* put an end to suffering and pain.

3) Thirdly, there is the assertion (which is certainly central to the Bible's teaching) that God is love. Presumably, therefore, he would *want* to stop it.

If any one of these three things were untrue, there would not be a theoretical or philosophical problem: if pain were unreal, if God were not almighty, or if he were not love. But if these things *are* true, then we come back to that persistent question, 'Why?'.

In Luke 13, people brought to Jesus' attention two disasters which had recently occurred, one being a human act of barbarism and the other a terrible accident. In the first, Pontius Pilate gave the order for the cold-blooded slaughter of a group of pilgrims even while they were worshipping in the temple, and in the other, a tower fell on a crowd in Siloam killing 18 people. They told Jesus about these things, and perhaps they were really raising with him this big issue: how can all that you're preaching be true when things like that happen?

And of course the list is a long one. How can you believe in God when there are earthquakes and typhoons? Can you watch 'Schindler's List' and still believe in God? What place is there for faith in a world which has experienced Hitler, the holocaust and Hiroshima? And the issue is just as real and intense when it's one person you love who suffers, as when it's a large number at one time.

Having then posed the problem, let us consider three questions:

- What explanation can Christianity give?

- What credibility can Christianity have?

- What help can Christianity offer?

What explanation can Christianity give?

A Christian response to this issue highlights two important things. The first is the link between suffering on the one hand and human sin on the other. The second is the fact that the world operates in terms of certain 'laws of nature' which are essential for life but which also entail the possibility of hurt.

The Bible describes the world God created as perfect in every way, and says that it was when human beings used their free will to rebel against God and disobey him that sin and suffering came into the world. And it is clear that a great deal of the suffering which plagues the world and seems to call into question belief in a good God is really in fact the direct consequence of sin.

People said, for example, about Auschwitz and Ravensbruck and the other Nazi concentration camps of the second world war, 'Where is God in all of this? If there is a God, why doesn't he put an end to it all?' But of course God has given us free will. Human beings are not just robots who are programmed to act in a certain way. We can choose which way to go. That is what makes us human; that is the way God has made the world; and, difficult as it may sometimes be to say it without seeming callous, we have to say that it is 'not on' to blame God for the evils which human beings perpetrate against one another.

If a drunk driver injures or kills someone, then it may be understandable that grief-stricken people cry out against God for 'letting it happen', but it wasn't actually God's fault. He has given us free will; he has given people the ingenuity to develop motor cars, and so on; and he has made the world in such a way that there are certain laws of nature.

James S. Stewart,[5] during a television interview *Why I Believe*, drew an illustration from the rugby field. He pictured a winger sprinting towards the goal line, with the opposing full-back coming across to cut him off; how wonderful for the player with the ball if the touch-line should suddenly move back a few yards and let him pass! But that can't happen; there wouldn't *be* any game of rugby if that kind of thing happened. He said, 'It's on the absolute rigidity of the touchline that the whole game depends. And that's true of the game of life.'

Mind you, that's not all he had to say. The interviewer asked 'Isn't that too intellectual to help?', and Dr Stewart went on to say that what the sufferer needs is not an intellectual explanation but a victory, which means a presence: 'and I should tell that person that God is in this experience with him or her, and he or she is in this thing with God'.

But our point is that the world as it is contains the possibility of suffering because of the fact that we human beings have been given free will and because the world 'works' according to certain 'laws of nature'.

One of the most awful tragedies of recent times in Britain happened at Aberfan where coal dust enveloped a school, suffocating 116 children and 28 adults first thing one ordinary school morning. Someone who contributed to the subsequent appeal fund wrote in a letter to the press, 'I raged against God, but then I realised that it had happened because of man's greed and incompetence' (which is what the official enquiry concluded). It has been suggested that as much as 95% of the sufferings of human beings are connected with human sin and selfishness.

I sometimes visit a middle-aged member of our congregation whose life story has been a catalogue of troubles. His father was one of our senior elders, who had been a member of the church choir for very nearly 50 years when he suffered a stroke; he wasn't able to speak after that (although sometimes he could *sing* some words). His wife devotedly looked after him and their son for many years before her own death. The younger son was lost at sea, and this older son has for many years been paralysed as a result of multiple sclerosis, as well as suffering the break-up of his marriage. It is the sort of family which has suffered so many disasters that it is hard to imagine many more that could come to them.

During one visit, this man said slowly in the course of conversation, 'The one thing that really bothers me is...' – I braced myself, expecting some expression of the sheer unfairness of it all, and of the big question about how anyone can believe in a God who allows such things to happen. In fact, what he said was: 'The one thing that really bothers me is all these murders and crimes.' He was more bothered about man's inhumanity to man than about the disasters which have crowded in to his own life.

He often makes me think. For one thing, he exemplifies the observation that often the people who do the suffering are not themselves the ones who raise the question about God's power and love, and how to reconcile the two. What mystified him was not the sufferings of his own life or the actions of God, but the cruelty of so many human beings.

No easy answers

However, that still leaves the other kinds of suffering. There are some kinds of suffering which clearly are *not* connected with human choices. One thinks of the droughts which afflict some parts of the world, the earthquakes that convulse other areas, and the trauma of babies born with severe handicap which can't be attributed to any human *fault*. Some instances of suffering seem to have nothing to do with human sinfulness or selfishness, and it would be insensitive and cruel to imply that someone who is suffering must have done something to 'deserve' it. The book of Job is a biblical protest against such easy equations.

In the passage we cited from Luke 13, we find Jesus asking, 'Do you think that these Galileans were worse sinners than all the other Galileans because they suffered this way?... Or those eighteen who died when the tower in Siloam fell on them – do you think they were more guilty than all the others living in Jerusalem?' He answered both questions by saying, 'I tell you, No!' It isn't as simple as that. If we ourselves suffer some trouble, there is no need for us to torture ourselves with the question, 'What did I do to deserve this?'; so far as the sufferings of others are concerned, we should avoid being 'Job's Comforters' by saying it must be because of something they have done.

One consideration which is sometimes brought in to give some kind of meaning to bad things that happen is the fact that good results have often come from bad experiences. Indeed, a famous New Testament text gives expression to the conviction of the apostle Paul that in all things God works for good (Rom. 8:28). Peter similarly counselled his readers about present trials: 'These have come so that your faith – of greater worth than gold, which perishes even though refined by fire – may be proved genuine' (1 Pet. 1:7).

The Old Testament character Joseph gave classic expression to the point when he said to his brothers who had hated him and maltreated him: 'You intended to harm me, but God intended it for good' (Gen. 50:20).

Hudson Taylor was the founder of the China Inland Mission (now the Overseas Missionary Fellowship), and I was interested to find a statement of this kind in his biography: 'he was impressed by the fact that every important advance in the development of the Mission had sprung from or been directly connected with times of sickness or suffering'.[6] The biographers, to finish the quotation, actually wrote: 'times of sickness or suffering which had cast him in a special way upon God' – which makes the point that it is our response and reaction to trials that makes the difference. But Taylor's experience is a practical illustration of how good can be brought out of evil.

One of the most helpful pastoral illustrations is one related by James Martin:

> The traditional manner of making a Persian carpet may provide an apt illustration. It is erected vertically on a frame and on one side a number of boys are seated at different parts of the carpet and at different levels. On the other side is the master weaver. He calls out instructions to the boys and they each weave in their part of the pattern according to the guidance received from a man whose face they cannot see. As the boys are able to see it, the design of the carpet is a complete mess, merely a collection of blotches and unsightly blobs. Looking at it from their viewpoint, it is hard to imagine that there is any sense about what each individual is having to do. Theirs, however, is the wrong side from which to judge. When, at the end of the day's work, they get down from their stools and walk round to the master's side, they can see that there *is* a pattern being worked out, a thing of intelligence and beauty.[7]

These things are true; good *can* sometimes come from things that seem to be evil and highly undesirable. So said the words of a prayer found in the clothing of a dead child at Ravensbruck concentration camp:

> O Lord, remember not only men and women of good will, but also those of ill will. But do not remember all the suffering they have inflicted on us; instead, remember the fruit we have borne because of this suffering – our fellowship, our loyalty to one another, our humility, our courage, our generosity, the greatness of heart that has grown from this trouble.[8]

At a lesser, more 'ordinary' level, why do we give young children the freedom to walk unsupported or to ride a bike, when these activities may entail pain for them? We allow it for the sake of the greater good of their being able to walk or cycle. And no doubt some of the things that happen are allowed by God for the sake of some greater good, whether we can understand it at the time or not. The child may blame the parent for his grazed knees, but later he will be thankful for the freedom that enabled him to learn to cycle.

However, that still does not explain why such things happen in the first place. We have sought to draw together some of the things Christianity can say on this issue, but it must also be said that, at the end of the day, we do not know all the answers. Sometimes we simply have to say we don't know why God allows certain things to happen. Christians do not claim to know all the answers to all the questions which might be asked. Even after everything has been said that can be said, there remain puzzles, problems and perplexities.

And *is* this a barrier to belief in God? This is our second question. If we cannot give a full and complete account of the reasons for the existence of suffering, can we still believe in God? Or should we abandon faith? Is suffering an insurmountable barrier?

What credibility can Christianity have?

When we come to consider the credibility of Christianity, we might begin with the assertion that the question is not whether Christianity can supply all the answers to all the questions, but whether, within the confines of our presently limited understanding, it can give a better explanation than other systems and beliefs can.

In this connection, consider some words of Professor John Baillie. Looking back to his student days, he recalled an essay he had written for his philosophy teacher. In it, he criticised a certain widely-held view, and when he received the essay back, he found that the teacher had written in the margin: 'Every theory has its difficulties, but you have not considered whether any other theory has less difficulties than the one you have criticised.'[9]

C. S. Lewis made the same point when he wrote, 'The question is whether any hypothesis covers the facts so well as the Christian hypothesis.'[10]

There *are*, as we have admitted, difficulties that remain, unexplained things that happen in the world, but our claim is that Christianity makes better sense of the facts than any other explanation.

Suppose you had a set of cards, and each of them had a musical note drawn on it, and you then threw them up into the air and went away; and suppose you then came back later and found them all arranged in such a way as to make a melody, let alone a harmony, let alone a fugue. Wouldn't you say, 'A musician has been here'? You would never believe that such a result could have come about by chance. What's more, even if you noticed a few discords, you would still conclude that a musician had been at work.

Like all such illustrations, this one has its limitations, but it brings home the challenge as to whether any alternative to belief in a caring God makes sense. Later we will consider Christianity's challenge to the unbeliever: what are they asking us to believe – that everything came about by blind chance? How are we to account for so much *goodness* in the world? If it is true that, so many millions of years ago, we were all at the level of the beasts, if we have simply evolved in some random manner, if the famous clockmaker of Paley's story is, as Richard Dawkins says, a *blind* watchmaker, then how are we to account for the heights of unselfishness and self-sacrifice to which human beings have sometimes risen? History tells the stories of many people who have sacrificed much for the sake of other people. I think, for example, of Maximilian Kolbe, a priest imprisoned at Auschwitz, who, according to a newspaper report, 'asked to replace another prisoner because this other man, Franciszek Gajowniczek had a wife and children. Three weeks later, the priest was killed with a carbolic acid injection as he lay naked in an underground cell.'[11] Many such stories of tremendous heroism could be told, and the challenge for the unbeliever and the materialist is: on your presuppositions, how can such things be accounted for?

Many years ago Bertrand Russell wrote a book called, *Why I Am Not A Christian.* If we were to turn the tables and write something called, *Why I Am Not An Atheist,* the very existence of goodness would be one of the reasons. True, there are things which are unexplainable in the meantime, but if we were to draw the conclusion that there is no God, then too there would be many things that would be unexplainable. C. S. Lewis went to far as to say provocatively that atheism is too simple an idea:

> in the very act of trying to prove that God did not exist – in other words, that the whole of reality was senseless – I found I was forced to assume that one part of reality – namely my idea of justice – was full of sense. Consequently atheism turns out to be too simple. If the whole universe has no meaning, we should never have found out it has no meaning; just as, if there were no light in the universe and therefore no creatures with eyes, we should never know it was dark. Dark would be a word without meaning.[12]

Christians believe that, even at this theoretical level, and even with the unexplainable things, it still makes more sense to believe in God than to reject belief.

This is not merely a way of saying that Christianity helps us to make the best of a bad job, as if it is a rather poor account of things but it is the best we've got! Christians would claim that there is much more to Christianity than that, but it remains true that Christians would press the issue of whether, even when we admit that we do not know all the answers, any other theory or philosophy can give a better account of things as they are.

This challenge could be expressed firstly in the form of a moving personal testimony, and secondly in the form of a direct challenge to those who reject the way of faith.

Arthur John Gossip preached a particularly moving sermon shortly after the death of his wife. The elders of Beechgrove Church in Aberdeen had it printed in pamphlet form, and it was later included in a volume of Gossip's published sermons. He said, 'I do not understand this life of ours' – which is a significant statement in itself. He did not claim to know all the answers; in fact, he candidly admitted that he did not, and the sincere Christian will not claim to be able to answer all the questions that can be asked. But Gossip went on: 'But still less can I comprehend how people in trouble and loss and bereavement can fling away peevishly from the Christian faith. In God's name, fling to what?' And he added, reflecting his own loss, 'Have we not lost enough without losing that too?'[13]

This is part of the Christian challenge to unbelief. We cannot answer all the questions, we do not have everything neatly tied up, but we would claim that, even with all the presently unanswerable questions, the way of faith gives a better account than anything unbelief can offer.

The other part of the challenge to unbelief is to pose the question of whether that way leads to greater benefit for the people of our world, and it is interesting to find this challenge addressed to postmodernism in a recent book:

> Against an insolent postmodern Gospel that dares to proclaim liberal democracy as the realized 'end' of human history, Derrida protests: '...never have violence, inequality, exclusion, famine and thus economic oppression affected so many human beings in the history of the Earth and of humanity... no degree of progress allows one to ignore that never before, in absolute figures, have so many men, women and children been subjugated, starved or exterminated on the Earth'.[14]

What indeed are the fruits of atheism? This subject will be considered later in this book, but even in connection with this barrier of suffering, we pose the question of which way – the way of Christ or the way of unbelief – leads to the greatest blessings for the world. Christianity's record has not been all good; this has to be admitted (we return to the issue in chapter 9). Nor does Christianity claim to hold any monopoly on goodness; it rejoices in goodness, wherever it is found. But the challenge is to consider whether, in today's widespread rejection of Christianity, we are in fact creating a better world for ourselves and those who come after us.

However, all of this may sound too theoretical and abstract, and we must come to a third consideration:

What help can Christianity give?

Does Christianity in fact help people to cope with suffering? Does it make any difference? This is the practical issue, for suffering is not merely a philosophical issue. The story is told of a man who saw a small boy running across a concrete path which the man had just left to harden. Observing the footprints in the concrete, he shouted angrily at the boy. Later an amused neighbour asked if he hadn't always said that he loved children. His response was, 'Yes, but I love them in the abstract, not in the concrete'!

Our concern here is not with Christianity's response to suffering as an abstract issue, but rather the question of whether it – or rather 'He', because Christianity is not primarily a system of belief, it is Christ himself – can give any concrete help, for this is an intensely practical issue, and if faith in Christ does indeed help people to cope, then that is worth considering. It is not a case of 'any port in a storm', nor are we advocating a placebo-type religion. It is worth considering whether the truth claims of Christianity are well-founded. That issue of truth comes first, but 'the

Christian is not ashamed that these beliefs meet his need any more than he is ashamed to eat food because it meets his physical need. The fact that these beliefs meet a need does not by itself prove they must be false.'[15]

Christianity's practical answer to suffering concerns a past event, a future hope and a present help, all of them centring on the person of Jesus Christ.

A past event

The past event is of course the cross of Jesus Christ. Christianity's answer to the problem of suffering centres on the cross of Christ. Among other things, that cross tells us that God has not remained aloof from human suffering.

We said that the question 'Why?', as well as being a human question, is a biblical question. It is also true that the centre of the Christian gospel concerns a 'Why?'. When Jesus hung in agony on the cross, he cried out, 'My God, my God, why have you forsaken me?' (Mark 15:34; Jesus was using words from the 22nd Psalm, which we quoted earlier in this chapter).

Professor T. F. Torrance has written:

> If I did not believe in the cross, I could not believe in God. The cross means that, while there is no explanation of evil, God himself has come into the midst of it in order to take it upon himself, to triumph over it and deliver us from it.[16]

The story of Jesus Christ tells us of God's action to come right into the world and redeem our humanity from the inside. Part of the glory of Christianity's answer is that it centres in a voluntary act of sacrifice which involved suffering.

An old story tells of multitudes of people gathered at the end of time before God's throne. The voice of a young girl rose from the crowd. 'How can God judge us? How can he know about suffering?' She ripped open a sleeve to reveal a tattooed number from a Nazi concentration camp. Similar things were shouted out by a black boy with a rope burn on his neck, a girl who had carried the stigma of illegitimacy all her life, and others. They agreed that God had led a rather sheltered life and had no right to judge them. They chose spokesmen, who conferred and agreed that before God could judge them, he must be sentenced to live on earth as a human being. And – let the legitimacy of his birth be doubted; give him a task so difficult that even his family would think him crazy; let him suffer betrayal by friends; let him suffer injustice; let him die a lonely and painful death. As each of the spokesmen announced his portion of the sentence, loud murmurs of approval went up from the great throng, and when they had finished there was a long silence. Those who had spoken their judgement of God departed. Nobody said anything. Nobody moved. For suddenly everybody realised – God had already served his sentence!

What's more, the amazing claim of the Bible is that these things were not forced on Jesus, but rather that he *chose* to undergo such agonies. For example, when the hostile crowd came to arrest him, and when he rebuked one of his disciples for wielding a sword, his words were: 'Do you think I cannot call on my Father, and he will at once put at my disposal more than twelve legions of angels? But how then would the Scriptures be fulfilled that say it must happen this way?' (Matt 26:53). Again, in the famous passage where he described himself as the Good Shepherd, Jesus spoke about laying down his life, only to take it up

again. He went on, 'No-one takes it from me, but I lay it
down of my own accord. I have authority to lay it down and
authority to take it up again' (John 10:18). Such claims are
remarkable, and they typify the Bible's assertion that Jesus
was not a helpless victim but one who, in love, gave his life
for the salvation of others.

Part of the practical response of Christianity to the
'problem' of suffering is to point to the sufferings of Jesus
Christ. As the Scottish Paraphrase puts it:

> Though now ascended up on high,
> He bends on earth a brother's eye;
> Partaker of the human name,
> He knows the frailty of our frame.
> In every pang that rends the heart,
> The Man of sorrows had a part;
> He sympathises with our grief,
> And to the sufferer sends relief.

A future hope

Another element in the practical answer that Christianity
gives concerns a future hope. It holds out the promise of a
time when everything will be made clear. Then the things
which we can't understand meantime will fall into place,
and we'll say, *'That's* why certain things happened.'
Another hymn-writer described it in these terms:

> I'll bless the hand that guided,
> I'll bless the heart that planned,
> When throned where glory dwelleth
> In Immanuel's land.[17]

This is another thing about how Christianity enables people to cope. If we trust with Romans 8:28 that in all things God works for the good of those who love him, if we believe with the Psalmist that 'The Lord is King for ever and ever' (Ps. 10:16), if we believe that through trials our faith, of greater worth than gold refined in the fire, may be proved genuine (1 Pet. 1:7) – then we will have strength for today and bright hope for tomorrow.

A present help

That brings us to the third element of Christianity's answer: a present help. The God who sent his Son to go through the experience of Calvary is the God who promises to be with us always, and many people have testified to knowing his strength in a special way in times of stress and trouble.

In Galatians 2:20 Paul described the essence of the Christian life in personal terms: 'I have been crucified with Christ and I no longer live, but Christ lives in me. The life I now live in the body, I live by faith in the Son of God who loved me and gave himself for me.' That verse speaks of a warm personal relationship with Christ; it reminds us that Christianity is far more than a philosophy or a moral code or a body of theology. It is much more wonderful than that. It is about a personal relationship of faith and love with a God who loves us and whose Word says, 'Cast all your anxiety on him because he cares for you' (1 Pet. 5:7).

One of the Psalmists even went so far as to state, 'It was good for me to be afflicted' (Ps. 119:71). These are not the words of an unbalanced masochist, but of one who expresses a wonderfully positive way of looking at life's trials and adversities. As he looked back, he even thought, 'Before I was afflicted I went astray, but now I obey your word' (Ps. 119:67). Often, people think it is the other way round; people may say, 'Everything was fine and I believed in God, and then this dreadful thing happened to me and I came to feel that such afflictions call into question the faith I once so easily accepted.' But the Psalmist's outlook is very different. He tells us from experience that there are lessons which can be learned in the time of adversity. No-one in their right mind desires trouble, but the Bible speaks of the transforming presence of Christ even *in* the time of trouble.

Paul tells of a distressing trouble he had. He doesn't spell out what it was, but it was evidently something which troubled him greatly. And he did what the Bible would encourage anyone to do – he prayed about it. 'Three times I pleaded with the Lord to take it away from me' (2 Cor. 12:8). But the answer he heard from God was, 'My grace is sufficient for you, for my power is made perfect in weakness' (verse 9). Christianity offers no guarantee of the removal of all problems, but it does speak of a God who gives new strength (Ps. 23:3), and who promises, 'When you pass through the waters, I will be with you; and when you pass through the rivers, they will not sweep over you' (Isa. 43:2).

Finally, Job, who suffered many terrible afflictions, testified that it was actually through his trials that he came to clearer knowledge of God. Far from having some masochistic liking for suffering, he cried out to God from the depths of his agony. And at the end of it all, he would look back to the days when he had been healthy and wealthy, and reflect on how at that time he had 'religion', but it had been a second-hand kind of religion. He prayed, 'My ears had heard of you but now my eyes have seen you' (Job 42:5). Now that he had been through so much, so many slings and arrows that had assailed his soul and battered down his human defences, now he had come to a closer walk with God.

As the heading of this section has it, 'God is our refuge and strength, an ever-present help in trouble' (Ps. 46:1).

Notes

1.   Quoted in sermon by D. Macleod in *Princeton Seminary Bulletin*, V, 2 (1984), p.149.
2.   L. Weatherhead, *Why Do Men Suffer?* (SCM, London, 1935), p.81.
3.   Quoted in R. Zacharias, *A Shattered Visage* (Baker, Grand Rapids, Michigan, 1990), p.144.
4.   A. Huxley, *Brave New World* (Penguin, Harmondsworth, 1932), p.195.
5.   J. S. Stewart, *Why I Believe* (St Ninians, Crieff, 1963), p.12.
6.   Dr and Mrs H. Taylor, *Biography of James Hudson Taylor* (Hopper, London, 1965), p.337.
7.   J. Martin, *Suffering Man, Loving God* (Saint Andrew Press, Edinburgh, 1969), pp.50f.
8.   Quoted in *Pray Now 1995-96* (Saint Andrew Press, Edinburgh, 1995), p.19.
9.   J. Baillie, *Invitation To Pilgrimage* (Oxford University Press, London, 1942), p.15.
10. C. S. Lewis, *God in the Dock* (Fount, London, 1971), p.83.
11   Reported in *The Scotsman*, October 1971.
12. C. S. Lewis, *Mere Christianity* (Collins, London & Glasgow, 1952), p.42.
13. A. J. Gossip, *The Hero in thy Soul* (T&T Clark, Edinburgh, 1928), p.110.
14. R. Appignanesi & C. Garratt, *Postmodernism For Beginners* (Icon Books, Cambridge, 1995), p.170.
15. C. Chapman, *Christianity On Trial* (Lion, Berkhamsted, 1972), p.82.
16. T. F. Torrance, *Preaching Christ Today* (Handsel Press, Edinburgh, 1994), p.22.
17. A. R. Cousins (1824-1906) in 'The Sands of Time' (*Revised Church Hymnary*, Oxford University Press, Glasgow, 1929, no. 581).

Chapter 3

Raised on Scientific Method

For many people, science is a barrier to faith. The 1993 survey of barriers to belief showed that to many people science still seems to call into question the whole notion of faith in a transcendent, supernatural God. Some have re-interpreted 'God' as a kind of life-force, the ground of our being, a divine spark shared by all living things, but the idea that the God revealed in the Bible might be a real God seems to many to be a relic from an earlier era when we didn't know any better.

From its famous first four words ('In the beginning God') onwards, the Bible assumes (rather than argues) that the God who subsequently revealed himself in many and varied ways, is the God who made everything and who still sustains everything by his power. The Bible's teaching is not about a God who made the world, wound it up and left it to go along on its own. Rather it reveals a 'hands on' God, who is, as the New English Bible translation of Romans 11:36 says, the 'Source, Guide and Goal of all that is'.

For many, however, it seems that modern science has made such a faith untenable. The issue no doubt needs the attention of those who are scientifically trained and in that sense able to 'speak the language' and give a scientifically reasoned account of the faith they hold. However, it is an issue that impinges upon us all, whether we are scientists or not, and we need to consider this potential barrier to faith. One is encouraged by Archbishop William Temple's testimony, 'My ignorance of science is so profound as to be distinguished!'[1] But, whether we are scientists or not, we need to think about this issue, which many people say keeps them from believing. Is there a conflict between science and faith? Should science be seen as a barrier to faith?

Many people evidently think so, from the eminent Richard Dawkins of Oxford's Zoology Department, who says that he sees no room for God in his scheme of things, to, at the other end of the scale, the schoolboy's essay comment, 'The difference between science and religion is that science is material, and religion is immaterial'!

A television documentary about the beginnings of life on this planet included a comment by the presenter, explaining [sic] that in the past people had seen the need for belief in a Great Designer of the universe, but as science has probed further and further back in time, this was becoming unnecessary. This was the view that was expressed – and expressed with all the assurance of a taken-for-granted assumption that would only be questioned by some theological Luddite. Yet, as with so many such statements, there is a misrepresentation of both science and faith; as someone has written about that programme, 'The presenter was of course entitled to his opinion – but not his opinion masquerading under the guise of science. The way it came over was to give it all the backing of careful scientific investigation. This is misleading at best, manipulative propaganda at worst.'[2]

Yet it is taken for granted by many modern people; they would assume that you *either* take a scientific view of things *or* a religious view, but that you can't have both.

Scientists and faith

It is interesting, before going any further, to put all of this into some kind of historical context, because one of the remarkable things about the outlook we have described is that it ignores the fact that many of the great scientists have been and are men of faith. Consider the following list:

* Sir Isaac Newton, the famous discoverer of the law of gravitation, said, 'The most beautiful system of the sun, planets and comets could only proceed from the counsel and dominion of an intelligent and powerful being.'

* Thomas Edison spoke of the existence of a Supreme Intelligence as 'almost proved by chemistry alone'.

* Lord Kelvin went so far as to say, 'If you think strongly enough, you will be forced by science to believe in God.'

* The astronomer Kepler spoke of science as 'thinking God's thoughts after him'.

* The microbiologist Louis Pasteur said, 'Science brings man nearer to God.'

These quotations make the point that it has not always been assumed that there is a clash between science and faith in God. In James Denney's words:

[S]urely it should be plain to the religious, at all events, that they can have no quarrel with science. If God created all that is, whoever finds out anything about the world is finding out the truth of God... every man of science is in this sense a minister of religion.[3]

The Christian origins of science

Indeed it can be stated that science is really a child of Christian thought. This was the view of the historian Herbert Butterfield. It was from Christian teaching about the one God that there arose belief in the uniformity of nature, the belief that things are predictable: it's not as if today when you drop an object from your hand it will fall to the ground but tomorrow it may float in the air.

Again, Christian teaching about the transcendence of God, as a Being not identified with nature, so that the world is not God but the creation *of* God, meant that experimentation was justified. This would not have been the case under systems which regard matter as either divine or evil, for if matter were divine, it would be sacrilegious to interfere with it, and if it were evil, it would be wicked to do so.

Far from science and religion being in conflict, the truth is that science really started from Christian presuppositions. 'Thinking God's thoughts after him' is a fine statement of the original concern of science – to describe and give an account of the things we see and perceive around us. The Christian view is that this is God's world, and science is the investigation of God's world. Scientific study and Christianity are to be regarded as allies, not antagonists.

Clashes

Of course there have been some famous (and unfortunate) clashes between science and religion. When Copernicus set forth his theory that the earth moves round the sun and not vice versa, the church of his day opposed him vehemently; similarly with Galileo. Much controversy raged around Charles Darwin's 'The Origin of Species' which was published in 1859, and so many of these controversies have given people the idea that we must either believe the Bible or take a scientific view, but we can't do both.

Yet, so far as origins are concerned, the book of Genesis simply states, 'In the beginning God created the heavens and the earth.' It doesn't say *how* he did it; it doesn't spell it out in terms of the accepted science of the day in which it was written down – we might say thankfully, because then it would have been superseded long ago. It simply points to this cardinal fact that everything that exists owes its origin not to chance but to the great Creator God, who, as the rest of the Bible then goes on to say, has spoken to mankind in many and diverse ways, and finally in his very Son whom he sent into this created world.

This is the core of Christian belief, as repeated regularly in the Apostles' Creed: 'I believe in God the Father Almighty, Maker of heaven and earth...'.

In actual fact it might be pointed out that the idea that everything *could* have come about by chance is itself a statement of faith. It is intriguing to consider the words of George Bernard Shaw:

> The science to which I pinned my hopes is bankrupt. I believed it once. In its name I helped destroy the faith of millions of worshippers in the temples of a thousand

creeds. And now they look at me and witness the tragedy of an atheist who has lost his faith.[4]

He recognised that belief in chance is a matter of faith also. The Christian claim is that belief in the Creator is far more reasonable than belief in chance.

Chance

Indeed, we would turn the whole issue back on those who claim or assume that science is a barrier to faith and ask them: is it really credible that a world of such complexity and orderliness could have come about by chance? Various illustrations can be used to make the point:

- Would anyone believe that an explosion in a supermarket could accidentally produce a Christmas dinner with all the trimmings? Not likely!

- The astronomer Fred Hoyle asked: what are the chances of a whirlwind blowing through a junkyard and assembling a Boeing 747 from the pieces scattered about the yard? Everyone would say such a thing would be incredible, and if that's so, how can we be asked to believe that such an amazing world as this could have come about by chance?

- It has been calculated that the odds against the chance formation of the enzymes necessary for any life to exist would be ten to the power forty thousand – which is about forty pages of nothings.

- A professor of biology, seeking to describe the complexity of the human brain, said that it is like five hundred million telephone exchanges all connected properly. The connections possible are ten to the power one thousand three hundred million million million million!

The more Christians find out about the amazing complexity of the world, the more we stand in awe of the Creator of it all. With beautiful simplicity, Genesis 1:1 says, 'In the beginning God created the heavens and the earth', and throughout that first chapter it is God's creative word that brings everything into being: God *said* such-and-such and it was so; and the last verse of the chapter says, 'God saw all that he had made, and it was very good.'

Reverence for creation

The whole Bible bids us have reverence for this created order out of reverence for the Creator himself. Nobody should love this natural world more than Christian believers who trust and love the One who made it all. Joseph Addison brought it out poetically in his hymn (based on Psalm 19):

The spacious firmament on high,
With all the blue ethereal sky,
And spangled heavens, a shining frame,
Their great Original proclaim.
The unwearied sun from day to day
Does his Creator's power display,
And publishes to every land
The work of an almighty hand.

The end of the hymn says:

> In reason's ear they all rejoice,
> And utter forth a glorious voice,
> For ever singing as they shine,
> 'The hand that made us is divine'.[5]

'In reason's ear' – we are not invited to have some kind of blind faith which takes a leap in the dark; there may be much more to say than this hymn says, but it's true that creation itself proclaims the glory of God.

Science and scientism

Perhaps there are some believers who are haunted by a kind of fear of science, somehow afraid that science does or will render that faith irrelevant or unnecessary ('immaterial', as the schoolboy said). But there is no need to be afraid of the onward march of science, because all truth is God's truth, and science, properly understood, is the investigation of the realities of things around us. In a sense it is – or should be – a neutral thing; it has no vested interests, no hidden agenda; it is simply a matter of investigating the world as it is.

Alister McGrath has illustrated the point well in a quotation which goes beyond what the present (non-scientifically-trained) writer can follow in its points of detail, but which demonstrates a truly scientific attitude. Writing about the theory of relativity, Einstein said, 'If the red shift of spectral lines due to gravitational potential doesn't exist, then the general theory of relativity is untenable.'[6] What is interesting about these words for our present purpose is, in the words of Karl Popper, that

[h]ere was an attitude utterly different from the dogmatic attitude of Marx, Adler and Freud, and even more so from that of their followers. Einstein was looking for crucial experiments whose agreement with his predictions would by no means establish his theory; while a disagreement, as he was first to admit, would show his theory to be untenable. This, I felt, was the true scientific attitude.[7]

Einstein wasn't only interested in facts that would 'fit' his own theories; rather, he was intent on following truth, finding out how things actually are, how (as Christians believe) God has made things.

We need, after all, to distinguish between science and scientism. Science is about the investigation of the world around us, but scientism is an outlook which reduces everything to the level of the observable and which sees no need for the 'God hypothesis'. A human being is seen as little more than a collection of chemicals; the famous analysis says we contain enough fat for seven bars of soap, iron for one nail, seven spoonfuls of sugar, varying quantities of lime, phosphorus, magnesium, potash and sulphur – something like £1.85's worth of raw materials. It may be true that that's how we are made up – but it is not true that we're *nothing but* that.

This is an important distinction, and Christianity's problem is not with science but with scientism. Christianity claims that there are more things in heaven and earth than are dreamt of in the philosophy of those who take such a reductionist view.

Science, truly understood, only serves to increase our sense of wonder at the greatness of the Creator. An inscription at the entrance to the Cavendish Laboratory in Cambridge quotes the words of Psalm 111:2: 'The works of the Lord are great.' The more we discover about the world which God has made, the more we are led to say 'The works of the Lord are great' – and indeed to go on from there to say (as the Psalms also say), 'The Lord is great.'

Complementarity

Science need not be a barrier to faith; it can indeed be a stepping-stone to greater faith and a greater sense of wonder before the Creator.

Professor Charles Coulson illustrates from flowers. He quotes some poetic words of Wordsworth about a primrose, and then says that the scientist looks at it and sees 'a delicately balanced biochemical mechanism, requiring potash, phosphates, nitrogen and water in definite proportions'; someone else says, 'A primrose is God's promise of spring.'[8]

Which of these views is correct? Of course they both are. You don't have to choose between them. They are the same thing, seen from different perspectives.

Again, a diamond could be defined by a geologist as a piece of crystallised carbon with a hardness of 10, by a millionaire as a symbol of his wealth, and by a newly engaged couple as a token of their love for one another and their commitment to one another. And again it's not that one view is right and the others wrong. They're all true, looking at it from different angles.[9]

Science is good at describing and analysing things, but it would be a great thing if people would recognise the limitations of science. Dr Donald Bruce, Director of the Church of Scotland's Society, Religion and Technology Project, has posed the question, 'Have we been too spellbound by science's successes to use our common sense about its weaknesses?',[10] and the renowned Stephen Hawking concluded his best-selling book, 'A Brief History of Time':

> What is it that breathes fire into the equations and makes a universe for them to describe? The usual approach of science of constructing a mathematical model cannot answer the question of why there should be a universe for the model to describe. Why does the universe go to all the bother of existing?[11]

Similarly, Professor Steve Jones, Professor of Genetics at University College, London, said in his Reith lectures:

> Science cannot answer the question that philosophers – or children – ask: why are we here, what is the point of being alive, how ought we to behave? Genetics has almost nothing to say about what makes us more than just machines driven by biology, about what makes us human. These questions may be interesting, but scientists are no more qualified to comment on them than is anyone else.[12]

But this is what the Bible *is* about. These early chapters of Genesis are not principally about *how* the world came into existence, but *why* it exists and *who* designed it. And aren't these the most important questions of all? It's wonderful to find out all we can about the physical world around us, but behind all that there's the question of why things are as they are. If we were to ask how it is that we are considering these words just now, an answer could be given in terms of the wonderfully complex movements of our arm muscles and tendons which enable us to hold the book, our sustenance by good food, and so on. A different explanation would refer to our conscious decision to pick up the book and open it and read it.

One other thought-provoking illustration of this principle of complementarity comes from the literary field:

> Consider 'David Copperfield'. Open it at any page, say page 372. How did David come to be the man we find him there? If we have read the book so far, we will probably answer in terms of his youthful adventures, his upbringing, etc. However it is possible to give another account. This is in terms not of the narrative but of the author. In this second account, David is interpreted as a creature of Charles Dickens, conceived and set into a world of his own, in the pages of the book. Whereas the first account confines itself within the limits of the narrative and can make sense even if we deny that there is an author, the second steps outside the book and concerns itself very much with the author.[13]

Science can be seen as giving an account of the observable realities around us, and sometimes it does so without reference to any Creator. But the point is that the two accounts are not contradictory but complementary.

Scientific method

This principle of complementarity reminds us that the scientific approach to the study of anything at all needs to use the appropriate means. There is something strangely unscientific about the challenge which is sometimes posed: 'Prove to me scientifically that God exists!'

A 'filler' item in the 'Readers' Digest' told the intriguing story of a conversation in an army officers' club.

'I was raised on scientific method,' asserted a major who was an agnostic, 'and no-one has ever proved to me scientifically that God exists.' He swept the group with a challenging glance, and noticed that the chaplain had joined the group. The major started to apologise, but the chaplain responded, 'It's quite all right. As a matter of fact, I was interested in your problem which is very like a problem of my own. As you know, I was raised on theological method and no-one has ever been able to prove to me theologically that an atom exists'! I don't know whether the major was convinced, but the chaplain made a good point.

The truly scientific approach to anything is the one that will use the appropriate means. It would be very unscientific (apart from silly) to investigate a geometrical problem by seeking to utilise the rules of grammar, or, for that matter, to attempt to describe *David Copperfield* in mathematical terms.

Again, democracy is a wonderful thing, and there are no doubt times when a vote is the proper way of settling an issue, but there are other times when such a procedure would be entirely inappropriate and indeed unscientific. The schoolboy may have been very advanced in democratic procedures when he suggested that the solution to a dispute about whether a particular rabbit was male or female was, 'Let's take a vote', but he was somewhat lacking in scientific method.

So are those who clamour for what they call 'scientific' proof that God exists. Religious truth cannot be examined in a test-tube. Just as one approaches the study of grammar in terms of grammatical principles, and as one studies chemistry with the help of test-tubes and other laboratory equipment, so the appropriate – and, therefore, scientific – approach to God must be along the lines of *godly* method, which is personal; indeed God's great challenge for human beings is that they should make the experiment of faith.

Let me conclude this chapter with the fable of the mice and the piano. A family of mice lived inside an old piano. Music filled their lives, and they drew comfort from the fact that, above them and yet near to them, there was an invisible Great Player who could make this wonderful music. One day a daring mouse climbed up inside the piano, and found out how music was made. Wires were the secret – vibrating wires. They must all revise their earlier beliefs; only reactionary mice (if we can imagine such creatures) could continue to believe in the Great Player. Later another explorer found out about hammers, dancing and leaping on the wires. It needed a slightly more complicated theory to account for everything, but it all went to show that they lived in a mechanical and mathematical world. Gradually the unseen Player came to be regarded as a kind of myth, a notion they once held but had now left behind as belonging to their pre-scientific past. But the pianist continued to play the piano!

Notes

1. Quoted by N. McCulloch, *Barriers to Belief* (Darton, Longman & Todd, London, 1994), p.82.
2. S. Gaukroger, *It Makes Sense* (Scripture Union, London, 1987), p.71.
3. J. Denney, *The Way Everlasting* (Hodder & Stoughton, London, 1911), p.82.
4. From *Too Good to be True*, quoted by S. Gaukroger, op. cit., p.9.
5. *Revised Church Hymnary* (Oxford University Press, Glasgow, 1929), no. 10.
6. Quoted by A. McGrath, *Bridge-Building* (Inter-Varsity Press, Leicester, 1992), p.211.
7. Ibid.
8. C. A. Coulson, *Science and Christian Belief* (Collins, London & Glasgow, 1955), p.90.

9.   J. Young, *The Case Against Christ* (Hodder & Stoughton, London, 1986), p.70.

10. Dr Donald Bruce, audio-cassette, *Facing The Issues* (Church of Scotland Board of National Mission, Pathway Productions, Edinburgh,1995).

11. S. Hawking, *A Brief History of Time* (Bantam, London, 1988), p.192.

12. Quoted by D. R. Alexander in 'Science: Friend or Foe?', *Cambridge Papers* 4, 3 (1995), p.2.

13. D. Spanner, article in *Viewpoint* (Scripture Union), 26, p.7.

Chapter 4

Only One Way?

Another of the barriers to belief identified by the 1993 survey is typified by one respondent who said that all religions are 'too dogmatic in their assertion that their particular faith is the true religion'.

Ours is an age in which pluralism rules and tolerance is regarded as *the* great virtue. Yet Christians have indeed maintained that there is only one way of salvation; they have said that, while people may come to Christ in different ways, it is only through Christ that people can come to God. The Bible proclaims, 'There is one God and one mediator between God and man, the man Christ Jesus' (1 Tim. 2:5), and we are faced with the question of how to respond when people say that this apparently exclusive and even intolerant attitude on the part of Christianity is a barrier to its acceptance in a pluralistic world.

Another respondent gave expression to a point which must have occurred to many people at some time, namely, 'Believing in Jesus is in part an accident of birth; if I had been born in Saudi Arabia, I would believe in Muhammad.' We will comment on this later in the chapter.

It would be relatively easy to state and expound the Bible's teaching on these matters. It says that Christ is 'the

way, the truth and the life' (John 14:6), and it teaches that
there is salvation in no-one else but Jesus Christ, for 'there is
no other name by which people may be saved' (Acts 4: 12).
But how are we to 'defend' such emphases against the claim
that they are barriers to the acceptance of Christianity
today?

Some Christians would suggest that Christianity needs
no defence in this or any other area; if it is God's truth, it is
quite capable of speaking for itself – the point Spurgeon
made when he was asked how he would defend the Bible
and famously responded, 'Defend it? I would as soon defend
a roaring lion. Let it out; it will defend itself.' The Bible can
indeed speak for itself, and our concern is with how the
Bible's teaching relates to our situation today. What can be
said to those who question such an exclusive faith?

Pluralism

Our society is nowadays commonly described as a multi-
faith society. It is obviously true that there are
representatives in British society today of most religious and
non-religious viewpoints. Recent reports tell of a national
body instructing its staff to refer to the 'festive season' rather
than Christmas, on the grounds that the word 'Christmas'
might offend adherents of other faiths. This over-zealous
approach typifies many instances of contemporary
pluralistic political correctness.

What is not often realised or remembered is the fact
that less than four per cent of the population belong to one
of the other major faiths (mostly Muslims and Hindus, with
also some Sikhs, Jews and Buddhists), whereas surveys show
that approximately three-quarters of the population would
describe themselves as Christians (whether 'practising' or

not). We will be making the point that Christianity ought to be a tolerant religion, but when we are told that Christianity should be treated as just one among a number of religious systems, we may well respond by saying that, at the basic level of simple representation, this is unfair, since Christianity is foundational to our culture and is the (at least 'official' or 'nominal') religion of most people in Britain.

In reporting on some of these considerations, David Winter has suggested:

Statistically (if in no other sense) Britain is a predominantly 'Christian' society – overwhelmingly so, in fact. And it is only those who have a vested interest in undermining that cultural heritage who try to deny it. Significantly, the leaders of the other world faiths present in Britain are not among them. They accept, and for the most part approve, the view of Britain as a society built on Christian principles and beliefs. All they ask is that they should be accepted as full and responsible members of that society, and treated with respect and consideration... it is not narrow or racist to remind the people of Britain of their Christian heritage, provided it is done without rancour, meanness or discourtesy.[1]

Despite these considerations, however, it is commonly accepted that ours is a pluralistic society.

'Pluralism' is an attitude which does not simply accept the fact that there *are* many religions and belief-systems in society, but one which looks down on all attempts to claim exclusive truthfulness for any of these views. Pluralism views life as a large supermarket, in which all of the religions and philosophies are laid out on the shelves, and customers are at liberty to pick and choose as they will: a bit of this and a bit of that to make up your own personal religion.

In this scheme of things, tolerance is regarded as the paramount virtue; you've got to just accept others' right to their own views and not try to change them.

What is Christianity's answer to the charge that in such a pluralistic world, its claims are unacceptably exclusive?

In this chapter, we would make four statements about Christianity and pluralism:

* The world in which Christianity originated was a pluralistic world.

* Christianity ought to be a tolerant religion.

* Pluralism is illogical and potentially dangerous.

* Christianity is concerned with questions of truth.

1. First-century pluralism

It is interesting to consider the fact that words like those of 1 Timothy 2:5, 'There is one God and one mediator between God and man, the man Christ Jesus', were set down in a pluralistic world. It is not that our world is in this regard totally different from the world of the Bible.

A great deal of the *Old* Testament is about the battle against pluralism. The Israelites were often attracted to the idea that other peoples' religions, notably Baal-worship, should be accepted or even incorporated into their own religion.

And when we come to the world of the New Testament, we find that that world too was remarkably tolerant and pluralistic. So far as the Romans were concerned, people could more or less follow any religion so long as they paid lip-service to Caesar. The thing that puzzled and sometimes exasperated the political powers of these early Christian days was the stubborn refusal of the Christians to compromise with other religions.

In the second century, for example, there was the famous case of Bishop Polycarp, who was martyred in AD 155. The crowd in the arena cried out, 'Away with the atheists' – referring to the Christians, who refused to worship the *many* gods of the time. The contemporary records tell of a Roman official saying to Polycarp, 'What harm is there in saying "Lord Caesar" and in offering incense, and so on, and thus saving thyself?'

Eusebius's account goes on, 'He at first made no reply, but since they persisted he said, "I do not intend to do what you advise." Then, failing to persuade him, they began to use threatening words; and they pulled him down hastily, so that he grazed his shin as he descended from the carriage.' In the stadium, the Proconsul said to him, 'Have respect to thine age [he was in his eighties].... Swear by the genius of Caesar, repent, say "away with the atheists".' The courageous man looked out at the crowd in the stadium, waved a hand at *them* and said, 'Away with the atheists'! And when the Proconsul persisted in his attempts to get Polycarp to recant, to adopt the attitude of pluralism – by holding to his faith in Christ but not being so exclusive about it, by just saying the necessary words and being released, Polycarp answered:

> If thou dost vainly imagine that I would swear by the genius of Caesar, as thou sayest, pretending not to know what I am, hear plainly that I am a Christian. And if thou art willing to learn the doctrine of Christianity, grant me a day and hearken to me.[2]

Polycarp was being pressurised to accept a pluralistic outlook, and he was ready to accept death rather than yield to this pressure.

Michael Green, having studied the history of the early church, concludes, 'The pluralism of the first and second centuries AD was the greatest in extent and intensity the world has ever seen.'[3] The issue which faces us in our day is not a new one.

2. Christianity and tolerance

Our second statement is that Christianity is, or should be, a tolerant religion. It has to be admitted that mistakes have been made; Augustine, for example, thought that the words of Jesus' parable, 'Compel them to come in' (Luke 14:23) mean that we should literally compel people to give some kind of assent to Christianity.

But Christianity ought to be a tolerant religion, because we recognise that God has given people free will. Liberty of opinion and conscience is rightly a much-prized thing – perhaps something we take too much for granted. Persuasion is one thing, but there should be no attempt on the part of Christians to *force* others into acceptance of their faith.

We may draw out the implications of such an attitude of tolerance by setting out four principles:

a) Belief in the uniqueness of Jesus Christ and his gospel is not tantamount to believing that all other religions are totally wrong about everything. Paul spoke about God giving some enlightenment to everyone: 'Since the creation of the world, God's invisible qualities have been clearly seen, being understood from what has been made' (Rom.

1:20). Christians can happily acknowledge the fact that there are many good points in other religions. Belief in the sole sufficiency of Christ as Saviour does not mean denying that is so.

b) Belief in the uniqueness of Jesus Christ and his gospel does not entail any kind of cultural imperialism. Unfortunately faith and culture get so intertwined that people sometimes make the mistake of insisting on certain principles as non-negotiable when they are simply culturally formed. Christian evangelism concerns the proclamation of Christ, not the proclamation of our (western) ways as if they were superior to the ways of others. It is the point made by Hudson Taylor, who believed that Scripture and common sense taught that Christianity in China should not be a foreign thing; he aimed to win converts who were truly Christian, but also truly Chinese. Missionary work has not always been carried out in this manner.

There are many good and agreeable things about our cultural life, but on the whole, it might be said that western culture has little to brag about. An Islamic leader, Dr Kalim Siddiqui, who has lived in Britain for some time, was asked whether he thinks it possible for Muslim and Christian cultures to co-exist in this country. His candid reply was, 'Quite frankly, I don't think there is a Christian culture in this country. This is a post-industrial, secular culture where prostitution, gambling, homosexuality – everything mankind has regarded as evil – have been legalized.'[4]

c) Our third assertion is that belief in the uniqueness of Jesus Christ and his gospel should not lead to arrogance. At the end of this chapter, we will emphasise the point that, after all, Christianity is not the invention or discovery of Christians, as if they had done tremendously well and could claim great things for themselves. When the message of Christianity came home to Paul, he realised that there was nothing for him to boast about. Writing to the Romans, he would say, 'What happens now to human pride of achievement? There is no more room for it... because the whole matter is now on a different plane – believing instead of achieving' (Rom. 3:37; J. B. Phillips).

d) Fourthly, belief in the uniqueness of Jesus Christ and his gospel does not give any grounds for claims that Christians are 'better' than other people. Christianity should obviously be making people better, but it is not a matter of comparisons at all.

3. The illogicality and potential danger of pluralism

So far we have considered the fact that the world in which Christianity originated was a pluralistic world, and we have suggested that Christianity ought to be a tolerant religion. Our third general principle concerns the nature of this pluralism which is so popular today, allied as it usually is with sincerity of belief (which goes with tolerance in modern political correctness). People say that *all* religions, after all, lead to God; it's just that they take different routes – just as all the spokes of a wheel lead to the one hub. It doesn't matter what religion you follow as long as you are sincere. Such a view, however, is both illogical and potentially dangerous.

Its illogicality

It is illogical in the first place, because of the simple fact that many of the religions of the world are contradictory to one another. It is simply not true that they all say basically the same things, and therefore can be regarded as simply different routes to the same destination. Contradictory things cannot all be true. If you say coal is black, and I say 'No it isn't, it's white', we cannot both be right; and it's no use saying that so long as we both sincerely believe what we believe, then it's somehow true *for us*.

Michael Green asks:

> How can all religions lead to God when they are so different? The God of Hinduism is plural and impersonal. The God of Islam is singular and personal. The God of Christianity is the Creator of the world. Christianity teaches that God both forgives a man and gives him supernatural aid. In Buddhism there is no forgiveness, and no supernatural aid.[5]

The same point was made, although from a diametrically opposite point of view, by the famous Lord Russell in *Why I am not a Christian*:

> I think all the great religions of the world – Buddhism, Hinduism, Christianity, Islam and Communism – both untrue and harmful. It is evident as a matter of logic that, since they disagree, not more than one of them can be true.[6]

Before we even come to any assessment of the rightness or wrongness of the different religions, it simply doesn't hold water to say that they are all basically one, and that they are all heading the same way. Someone else has stated the point this way: 'We may sincerely believe that Dallas is in Africa, that the moon is made of cheese or that a Mars bar is a pub on another planet! But we would be wrong.'[7]

Its potential dangers

Secondly, we would suggest that pluralism is not only illogical, but also potentially dangerous. If a thing is not true, then the greater the sincerity with which it is held, the greater the danger.

Recently, when my wife was driving, the driver of another vehicle signalled for her to pull in. She thought that it was a police car, and wondered whether she had inadvertently exceeded the speed limit or passed a stop sign without stopping. It turned out to be another road-user who kindly informed her that one of the back wheels was wobbling. Sure enough, the wheel was slightly buckled – only slightly, but 'slightly' doesn't help much with buckled wheels! Until then we had sincerely believed that everything was fine with the car; we had no suspicion that there was anything wrong. But that sincerity made no difference whatsoever to anything; in fact the sincerity of that belief was very dangerous in that it might have led to real trouble on the road.

The more sincerely you believe something that isn't true, the more dangerous it may be. And when it comes to the issues with which 'religion' is concerned, we are talking about the most important issues in life. Religion is not just some inconsequential thing, as significant as whether you happen to like (say) bowls. Bowlers can be very enthusiastic and even wonder how the rest of us can get by without bowling. In fact we do manage quite well, and everybody knows that it really doesn't matter very much; if you fancy it, that's OK; if not, well that's OK too. But when it comes to spiritual matters, we are talking about things of the greatest possible importance – both for our lives in this world and for our eternal destiny. Nothing hangs on whether we like bowls or not, but everything hangs on the truth or otherwise of the Christian claim and our response to it.

If Christianity is *un*true, then the consequences are minimal – it means that many people have been, and are, basing their lives on a delusion, but it can hardly do them any harm. On the other hand, if the claims of Christianity are true, then the rejection of it (or of *him*, for Christianity really is Christ) will entail loss both in this life and in the life to come. We are told that Encyclopaedia Britannica published a 55-volume series called, *The Great Books of the Western World*. It brings together the most important ideas in law, science and philosophy. When the editor was asked why it was that the longest essay is about God, he replied, 'It is because more consequences for life flow from that one issue than from any other.'[8]

4. *Christianity and truth*

Our final point is that Christianity is concerned with questions of truth. We need to ask of any attitude or belief: is it true? This is not the same as saying, 'Is it true for you? Does it somehow appeal to you and ring bells for you?'

Consider this, from a newspaper-cutting about religious studies in a Scottish Academy: 'The main emphasis of any religious studies work is on the promotion of tolerance. Everyone's viewpoint is valid.'[9] Such a statement may sound attractive, it may be politically correct, it may exude tolerance – but it really won't do. A moment's thought will reveal that tolerance must have limits.

There are some people, for example, who have believed that it was their duty to kill other people. Are we simply to say, 'Well, everyone's viewpoint is valid'? Not so long ago, there were people who thought that white-skinned people were in some way superior to black-skinned people or brown-skinned people. Are we supposed just to say 'Well, everyone's viewpoint is valid; you've got to have tolerance'? When the pioneer missionary David Livingstone so vehemently opposed the slave-trade in Africa, should he have been told, 'But listen, it isn't for you to impose your views on others'? No, it may sound attractive in a way, but it won't do.

At the outset of this chapter we noted the view that belief in Jesus is in part an accident of birth: 'if I was born in Saudi Arabia, I would grow up to believe in Muhammad.' How are we to respond to such an assertion? Is it true? Perhaps. We might as well admit it's possible. Our background and upbringing no doubt play a very large part in making us the people we are.

But that does not affect the question of truth. We must still face the question of what the truth is. Once there was great controversy about the shape of the earth. Some believed that it was flat, while others believed that it was spherical. While the controversy raged, the residents of one village settled on a method of deciding the issue once and for all. They took a vote! The majority voted in favour of the view that the earth was flat – so that settled it!

But everyone would realise that their voting makes no difference to the question of the truth of the matter.

Christianity is concerned with questions of ultimate truth – indeed with the claim of Jesus Christ to *be* the truth – and there is no need for timidity on the part of Christians about this pursuit of truth. We made the point in relation to science that some Christians almost seem to be afraid of science and scientific investigation, but if Christianity's assertion is true – that all truth is God's truth – then there can be nothing to fear from the honest pursuit of that truth.

This points to the answer to the assertion that we might have been adherents of another religion if we had been brought up in some other part of the world. That is indeed possible, for our upbringing and cultural environment play a large part in making us what we are. But the question is the question of truth, not of culture. Whatever our background has been, we need to seek to divest ourselves of the conditioning factors in that background, and take as objective a look as possible at the issue of truth and the claims of Christ to be the truth.

We who are Christians do not adhere to Christianity because it is a nice story or a congenial philosophy, but because we have become convinced of the truth-claims of Jesus Christ.

Nor do we hold to Christianity because it is a useful thing. It was said of the world in which Christianity arose that all religions were equally true to the common people, equally false to the philosophers and equally useful to the state. But however useful it may be, the question is the question of truth. Christians believe that many beneficial results follow from Christian belief, but the beneficial results do not constitute the basis of our belief. It is a matter of being convinced of its *truth.*

That truth centres on the revelation that we believe God has given; Christianity is nothing if not a religion of revelation. It is the belief that God has made himself known in various ways and supremely in the person of Jesus Christ. Just as you can only know me if I open myself up to you, so God can only be known if he has made himself known to us. This is the fundamental thing about Christianity. God has revealed himself, and it is to the unique person of Jesus that we seek to point people.

The claim of Christianity is that Jesus is not a long-gone heroic figure who lived a good life, died a noble death and left a wonderful legacy of teaching and inspiration. In 1 Corinthians 15 Paul revealed that there were people even in these early days who had doubts about the central Christian claim that Jesus rose from the dead. Paul himself sought to have them work out the consequences which would follow if Jesus had remained dead. If that were the case, he said, there would be no faith ('your faith is futile' – v.17), no forgiveness ('you are still in your sins' – v.17) and no future ('those who have fallen asleep in Christ are lost' – v.18). He was not arguing that the consequences of a purely materialistic view are so awful that it just *must* be true, that in that sense we *need* to believe it all. Paul's faith and teaching were based on more solid ground than that, and in this same chapter he refers to the historical evidence of the appearances of the risen Christ and to his own personal testimony – 'last of all he appeared to me also' (v.8).

And as these materialists of Corinth were challenged to face up to the consequences of their outlook, so western materialists today need to be challenged about the implications of their secularism; this will be expanded in chapters 5 and 6. Similarly there is the challenge to find an alternative explanation which does justice to the facts in relation both to the historical events of the Easter story and to the contemporary realities of Christian experience. The existence of the Lord's day (Sunday), the production and amazing survival of the Lord's book (the Bible) and the continuing story of the Lord's people (the church) all speak powerfully for that which Christians believe is the foundation of them all, namely the resurrection of Jesus

Christ from the dead and his reality as a living Lord today. It is not that the Bible or the church explain the resurrection of Christ, but that the resurrection of Christ explains the existence of both the Bible and the church.

The claim that its Master is a living Lord is the thing that marks Christianity off from other religions and philosophies. That living Lord is making a difference in the lives of his followers. In one significant passage, Paul set down a list of the kind of people who 'will not inherit the kingdom of God' (1 Cor. 6:9): 'Neither the sexually immoral nor idolaters nor adulterers nor male prostitutes nor homosexual offenders nor thieves nor the greedy nor drunkards nor slanderers nor swindlers will inherit the kingdom of God.' He then added, 'and that is what some of you were'. Apart from being a statement of historical fact, that is a highly significant testimony to the transforming effect of the living Christ. Lives were being completely transformed. It was happening then; it has been happening ever since; it is happening still.

This chapter has been about pluralism. We have suggested that in fact Christianity originated in a pluralistic world, and it certainly ought to be a tolerant religion, but we have suggested that pluralism is illogical and potentially dangerous and that Christianity is ultimately concerned with the question of truth.

Some time ago, my wife was returning from a meeting in Edinburgh, and as she settled down for the two-hour train journey north, she casually said to a fellow-passenger, 'Are you going all the way to Aberdeen?' The answer she received caused her some consternation: 'No; all the way to London'!

And we conclude this chapter with some words of Dietrich Bonhoeffer: 'If you board the wrong train, it's no use running along the corridor in the opposite direction.'[10]

The important thing is to be on the right train.

Notes

1.   D. Winter, 'Just another world faith?', *Leading Light* 2,1 (1995), p.27.
2.   Eusebius, *Ecclesiastical History*, IV,15 (in ed. H. Bettenson, *Documents of The Christian Church*, Oxford, London, 1963).
3.   M. Green, *Evangelism Through the Local Church* (Hodder & Stoughton, London, 1990), p.75.
4.   Article in *Sunday Telegraph*, 3 November 1991.
5.   M. Green, *You Must be Joking* (Hodder & Stoughton, London, 1976), p.43.
6.   B. Russell, *Why I am not a Christian* (Watts & Co., London, 1927), p.9.
7.   S. Gaukroger, *It Makes Sense* (Scripture Union, London, 1987), p.31.
8.   R. Zacharias, *A Shattered Visage* (Baker, Grand Rapids, Michigan, 1990), p.12.
9.   Quoted in *Banffshire Journal*, 1990.
10. Quoted by R. Ferguson, *George Macleod* (Harper Collins, London, 1990), p.152.

Chapter 5

Bread Alone?

So far we have been considering barriers to belief presented by specific 'intellectual' issues – the existence of suffering, the advances of science and the exclusive claims of Christianity.

We turn now to other, more unconscious barriers which relate to 'the secular climate around us today, factors in the cultural air we all breathe which tend to suffocate faith'.[1] Many people, the 1995 report suggests, have not seriously considered the claims of Christianity, but have accepted the assumptions of a secular society, with its materialism, rationalism, pluralism, hedonism and permissiveness.

The title of this chapter comes from a verse in the book of Deuteronomy, a book that was written a long time ago in a world very different from our world. Yet in a remarkable way it still challenges our attitudes and assumptions as we enter the twenty-first century.

We have amazingly sophisticated means of communication today (faxes, e-mail, internet, etc.), but is there not a nagging doubt about whether we have anything worth communicating? We live in a world of ever faster and more comfortable transportation, but isn't there a question about whether we're really going anywhere?

Materialism

And what does Deuteronomy say? One of its most famous verses (8:3) says, 'Man does not live on bread alone but on every word that comes from the mouth of the Lord.'

That whole eighth chapter says to the people of Israel: a time will come when you are settled in your promised land, and you will have a higher standard of living than you would ever have thought possible – things will seem to be going well for you; be careful then not to become materialistic, egocentric, pleasure-seeking secularists, the proverbial self-made people who worship their own creator.

The writer of Deuteronomy was saying: material well-being has a way of making you think you're fine on your own. Verse 18 says, 'Remember the Lord your God, for it is he who gives you the ability to produce wealth.' And the chapter ends with a solemn warning: 'If you ever forget the Lord your God and follow other gods and bow down to them, I testify against you today that you will surely be destroyed.'

It is the same message as that which Jesus propounded when he said, 'Watch out! Be on your guard against all kinds of greed; a man's life does not consist in the abundance of his possessions' (Luke 12:15).

The story is told of a rich businessman who one day came upon a fisherman who was sitting by his little boat. The businessman asked, 'Why aren't you out fishing?', to which the fisherman replied that he had caught enough fish for that day. Not surprisingly, the businessman said, 'But why don't you go out and catch more than you need?'

When asked, 'What would I do with them?', he suggested that the fisherman would be able to sell them and get more money; eventually he would be able to buy a larger boat – possibly even a fleet of boats. 'Then,' the businessman said, 'You could be rich like me.' The fisherman asked, 'Then what would I do?', to which he received the reply 'Then you could sit down and enjoy life.' And the story ends with the fisherman saying, 'What do you think I'm doing now?'

The story pokes fun at what seems to be the principal motivating factor for so many people in our materialistic society. Ours is an age which needs to heed the warning of Deuteronomy 8 – even more than its original hearers did. We have a standard of living which is obviously very much higher than anything that could ever have occurred to these ancient people (even to our own grandparents). Within a fairly short time, we have come to take for granted foreign holidays, dishwashing machines, car phones, and so on.

And we *know* the truth of what Deuteronomy teaches – that wealth and prosperity have a way of turning us into self-sufficient materialists; so much of modern life seems to be based on the notion that you *can* live on bread alone.

Yet here it stands – the word of Scripture, underlined by Jesus himself: man cannot really *live* on bread alone. Many people seem to suppose that if they could only land lucky in the national lottery (or in some other way land a windfall), then everything would be fantastic in their lives. Yet at the same time we are hearing stories of misery and disillusion and even of people wishing they had never won all that money.

In September 1995 the Daily Record carried a report about a lottery winner who said that his £11.3 million win had ruined his life. 'He spoke for the first time yesterday about how his world has been turned upside down, and moaned: "I wouldn't recommend it to anyone. I never wanted millions. A few hundred thousand would have done nicely."' The Aberdeen *Press & Journal* told of another millionaire winner who said that there were times when he wished he had never seen the money; 'Life's such a drag now that I can afford anything I want.' The headline for this story read, 'Lottery man finds life so boring now.' It is paralleled by a headline in The Herald (13th June 1995): 'Record £22.5m win marred by dispute', with the sub-heading, 'Estranged wife attacks husband, demanding half his lottery share.'

If the much heralded national lottery has demonstrated anything, it has demonstrated the fact that satisfaction is not guaranteed by wealth.

Consider comedian Bobby Ball's reflection on his former life:

> Many men think that drinking, womanising, fighting and clawing their way up power mountains is the way that life should be lived. But they are wrong. I know because I have been there. If these people are truly honest with themselves and look deep into their hearts they will see that they are not truly happy, something is missing. The thing that is missing is God, because no-one can be truly happy until they have found him.[2]

A similar testimony is given by the athlete, Kriss Akabusi. In Edinburgh for the Commonwealth Games in 1986, he read a New Testament in his room, and he has written about his experience:

> When I opened up that Bible I was confronted with Jesus. All of a sudden there was a context to this guy. And this

guy said some powerful words: 'I am the way, the truth and the life', and, 'I will give you life in all its fullness.' I was in a situation where I had everything. I'd got much more than I needed, but it wasn't giving me happiness. There was no meaning and no purpose to my life. I was rushing around and trying to be famous – and I was getting famous. I was trying to get rich – and I was getting rich. But I wasn't very happy with my life or with my relationships.[3]

Secularism

The materialism we have been considering is one aspect of the secular attitude which has taken hold of so much of modern life. Many writers have described our huge shopping malls at the turn of the twenty-first century as symbols or icons of our time. This is so in a double sense: they speak literally of the materialism that prevails, and they speak symbolically of the pluralistic attitude of shopping for a personal system of values and beliefs – 'Pick 'n' Mix at the Pluralist Superstore'.[4]

Os Guinness gives an eloquent summary of our present situation:

Secularisation is the acid rain of the spirit, the atmospheric cancer of the mind and of the imagination. Vented into the air not only by industrial chimneys, but by computer terminals, marketing techniques and management insights, it is washed down in the rain, shower by shower, the deadliest destroyer of religious life the world has ever seen.[5]

At the beginning of this chapter we spoke about the air we breathe nowadays. Breathing is something we do unconsciously. We do not think to ourselves each morning, 'I must remember to keep breathing all day today.' We just do it, and it is only when we deliberately think about it that we become consciously aware of the process whereby we do all the time something on which our lives depend.

Similarly, in the area of thought, there are ideas around us 'in the air', as it were. Occasionally we are conscious of them (perhaps we welcome some theory or we object to something), but much of the time we are not particularly conscious of what we're breathing in at all. This has become all the more so, of course, in the twentieth century with the advent of virtually universal television, which smuggles all sorts of ideas into our minds, without our even being aware of it.

In another of his books, Os Guinness has described modernity as 'a new kind of worldliness that has sneaked up on us without our realizing it.... No persecutor or foe in two thousand years has wreaked such havoc on the church as has modernity.'[6]

He relates the fascinating story (told, he says, by Nikita Kruschev) about a time in the former USSR when there was a wave of petty thefts and the authorities had to place guards at all of the factories. Pyotr Petrovich worked at a timberyard in Leningrad, and one evening he left work with a wheelbarrow which contained a bulky sack with a suspicious-looking shape. The guard asked what was in the wheelbarrow, and Petrovich said, 'Just some sawdust and shavings.' The guard was not satisfied and told Petrovich to tip it out. Sure enough, it was a load of sawdust and shavings, so he was allowed to put it all back and go home.

The next evening, the same thing happened – another load of sawdust and shavings.

It happened every night that week, until the frustrated guard said, 'Petrovich, I know you. Tell me what you're smuggling out of here, and I'll let you go.'

And Petrovich owned up: 'Wheelbarrows, my friend, wheelbarrows.'[7]

Aspects of secularisation

Secularisation is reflected in many particular features of life today, and the returns sent in by the Church of Scotland Presbyteries about barriers to belief did in fact refer to several specific features of secularisation. Three things were mentioned with some regularity.

1) One was the secularisation of the media. Ardrossan Presbytery's report, for example, said, 'The media subtly undermine Christian beliefs and values, both by weak characterisation of Christians and by the representation of Christian morality as restrictive and old-fashioned.' (Interestingly, this point was mentioned in a 200-word section of the 10,000-word report, *Understanding The Times*, but on publication of the report, it was the principal section which attracted media attention and comment.) Television, in particular, has been described as 'the secular pulpit', and the message it proclaims is frequently a very different one from that which comes from the other kind of pulpits.

2) Another was the perceived secularisation of education. Religion, it was felt by many, is often marginalised as a minority interest, akin to a school's table tennis club or debating society – extra-curricular activities, but not part of the underlying basis of everything that happens in the school. In one region, it is reported that chaplains are asked not to mention Jesus!

3) The other specific illustration is the secularisation of Sunday. In Stirling Presbytery, a man in the fifty-plus age-group claimed that he believed in God, but he attended church infrequently – because 'I organise youth football on a Sunday'. This is a reminder that the problem (from the church's point of view) lies not so much with the young people in this matter as with the adult generation which organises such activities on Sundays. Such people, it may be suggested, have little conception of the possible consequences in depriving children of the positive influence of 'Sunday School', which, even if they themselves have forsaken the church, possibly played a larger part than they realise in forming whatever good and positive values they have.

These are three particular manifestations of secularism which were mentioned as barriers to belief.

But, important as these issues are, they may be likened to the sawdust and wood-shavings which Petrovich smuggled out in his wheelbarrow, while the wheelbarrow itself represents the whole scheme of thought and feeling that steals these other things out of the factory.

Part of the Christian task today is to seek to understand how today's people tick, and then to seek to find ways of commending the unchanging message of Christ crucified and risen to people whose attitudes have been unconsciously altered. Our world badly needs to hear what Deuteronomy 8 says – that 'man cannot really live on bread alone', that we need more than the material things of life, that it is tragically possible to gain the whole world and yet lose our souls (Mark 8:36).

Christianity's challenge to secularism

Deuteronomy 8:3 has both a negative and a positive aspect. It says negatively, 'Man does not live on bread alone', and that is followed by the positive assertion that man can live on 'every word that comes from God'.

This may give us a pointer to the need for such a double thrust today – negatively, a challenging of the assumptions of modern secularism, a kind of breaking up of the hard ground to prepare a way for the second thing – the sowing of the seed in the positive proclamation of the Christian message.

In this chapter, I would apply all of this to the area of meaning in life, and in the next chapter to the area of our need for some basis for morality. In doing so, we may be pressing questions which many people would rather leave unasked, and probing issues which many would rather ignore.

The question of meaning

One fifteen-year-old girl wrote a poem for her school magazine, in which she gave honest expression to a feeling which many people try to suppress if it ever rears its head. It may not be great poetry, but it expresses a real cry from the heart:

> To me the world is dances,
> pop and sherbet fizz,
> But underneath the icing
> What an awful hole it is.[8]

Many people would not state the issue as starkly as that or even think about it at all. But, painful or not, there are issues which need to be faced.

Could it even be that much of the noise and kerfuffle that characterise modern life is really a form of escapism, an effort to avoid facing up to serious questions and to make up for the emptiness of life? The irony is that Christians are sometimes accused of escapism and wishful thinking, while the secularists, who ignore 'religion', regard themselves as realists and pragmatists. We might well consider whether it isn't indeed the other way round. Is it not *un*belief, secularism, 'bread-alone' materialism, that is the real escapism and wishful thinking?

Zedekiah was the last king of Judah before the fall of Jerusalem in 587 BC. The Babylonian armies were advancing, and Zedekiah tried to escape, but he was captured. Writing about that attempted escape, one Old Testament scholar wrote, 'His flight, *like his life-long flight from reality*, could have only one outcome' (my italics).[9] Many people then and now would say that people who believe in an unseen world and pray to an unseen God are the escapists, the people who are seeking refuge from the harsh realities of life. Here, however, is a vigorous challenge to such an outlook. Christians believe that it is the Zedekiahs of today who are running from reality. After all, true realism in any sphere involves taking account of all the data, and most of all in this question of ultimate meaning and destiny.

In a graduation address, Sir Thomas Taylor, one-time Principal of Aberdeen University, suggested that it is with eagerness that we clutch at the various 'explanations' (Oedipus complex, and so on) which are held to explain away our sense of responsibility. 'This,' he suggests, 'is why atheism has a perennial appeal; it is wishful thinking in its most enticing form.'[10] This is his description, not of Christianity, but of atheism: *wishful thinking in its most enticing form.*

Christianity's challenge to people today is that they should consider whether they are in fact running away from the awkward and sometimes disturbing fact that life for them really doesn't have any meaning. The endeavour to live for bread alone, without any regard for 'every word that comes from the mouth of the Lord', leads to meaninglessness.

Shakespeare's tormented Othello soliloquizes about his love for Desdemona; Iago has led him to doubt his beloved's faithfulness, and we hear him saying:

> But I do love thee; and when I love thee not
> Chaos is come again.[11]

The Christian claim is that life is always going to be chaotic if God is not given his rightful place *in* our lives. Without the sense of purpose and direction which comes from faith in and commitment to Jesus Christ, life is little more than the frantic effort to roll a massive stone to the top of a hill, watch it roll down again, and then repeat the exercise, time after time, endlessly and pointlessly.

Ravi Zacharias, in one of his books,[12] refers to the old nursery rhyme about the poor old Duke of York who had ten thousand men. He marched them up to the top of the hill, and then marched them down again! And it goes on:

> When they were up they were up,
> And when they were down they were down,
> And when they were only half-way up,
> They were neither up nor down.

As Zacharias says, 'If it were not for the melody of this rhyme, its information quotient would not exactly stir the intellect.' He then goes on to quote the fairground analogy of Joni Mitchell's song:

> And the seasons, they go round and round
> And the painted ponies go up and down –
> We're captives on a carousel of time.

Is that how it is – just up and down, and round and round, for however many years, until the curtain comes down on this sad farce?

I vividly remember the sadness I felt as an undergraduate when I read an anonymous letter in the Edinburgh University's 'Student' newspaper in 1967, under the heading, 'An old fogey's lament'. The aged writer had been a student at the university, and would pass on the benefits of his experience to the younger generation of students. The letter is worth quoting at length as a particularly candid expression of the chaos that life can become without something to give it meaning:

> All our life long, we have been living in dread of creeping old age and death. Now that we have reached the senile state, we can assure you, young fellows, that it isn't at all funny. Our genitors would have saved us an awful lot of misery if they had refrained from pulling us out of nothingness, or dust as the Bible puts it, only to force us back to where we came from, after this perfectly useless sojourn in a mad world. Only when you reach the last stage of your earthly passage do you begin to realise that life is just a senseless, useless, stupid adventure, seeing that once you are dead, you revert back to the very same

condition of non-existence as if you had never lived at all. Dreams and future planning create the illusion that life is worth living and struggling for. And it is only when you reach the terminus that you begin to realise that life is tomfoolery from beginning to end. Biologists, hygienists, eugenists are boasting that they have substantially increased the normal life span. So what? Whether you pop off after 100 minutes, 100 hours or 100 years of earthly existence, what difference does it make?

It is clearly a sad letter from any point of view. This 'old fogey's' expression of meaninglessness is a particularly articulate and possibly extreme one – yet the Christian claim is that the view expressed in these words is indeed 'The Real Face of Atheism' (the subtitle of Zacharias' *A Shattered Visage*). This is how it is – *if* the assumptions of atheistic secularism are right.

All of this represents what we called the negative side of Deuteronomy 8:3. It says that people cannot live on bread alone; materialism is a dead end.

A positive message

Its positive message is that people *can* live a fulfilled life if God is given his proper place and life is lived in relation to him. God has given us his Word, his message – something which does give meaning and significance to our lives in this world, something which delivers us from the fervent attempt to avoid thinking about such things.

The good news is that Jesus Christ, who was crucified but who conquered death, can come into people's lives and give them a sense of meaning and purpose, assure them that they matter to God, who is not some impersonal force but a loving Father who gave us life in the first place, who wants to enrich our lives in this world and give us all things richly to enjoy, and who wants to bring us to eternal life to be with him forever

Atheism isn't just taking sawdust and wood-shavings from the factory. It's worse than that – it is stealing wheelbarrows right under people's noses. It is taking away the very basis on which meaning can be found. Man cannot really live on bread alone. We need the message that comes from God. It is Christ who gives meaning to life and delivers people from despair and hopelessness.

Notes

1. *Understanding The Times* (Saint Andrew Press, Edinburgh, 1995), p.15.
2. B. Ball, *My Life* (Spire, London, 1993), p.209.
3. K. Akabusi, *On Track with the Bible* (Bible Reading Fellowship, Oxford, 1995), p.9.
4. G. Cray, *The Gospel and Tomorrow's Culture* (CPAS, Warwick, 1994), p.17.
5. Os Guinness, *The Gravedigger File*, quoted by G. Cray, ibid., p.12.
6. Os Guinness, 'Mission in the face of modernity' in *The Gospel in the Modern World*, ed. Eden & Wells (IVP, Leicester, 1991), p.86.
7. Ibid., p.85f.
8. In 'Choose Life' (unpublished), by Sandy Gunn.
9. D. Kidner, *The Message of Jeremiah* (IVP, Leicester, 1987), p.126.
10. T. Taylor, *Where One Man Stands* (Saint Andrew Press, Edinburgh, 1960), p.24.
11. W. Shakespeare, *Othello*, III. iii. 90 (Tudor Edition, London, 1951).
12. R. Zacharias, *A Shattered Visage* (Baker, Grand Rapids, Michigan, 1990), p.76.

Chapter 6

Withered Fruit

In the last chapter, we have been concerned with the lack of a sense of meaning which characterises modern living in the affluent parts of the world. If meaning were to be found in material possessions, then western society today ought to be filled with people who have a rich sense of meaning and fulfilment in life. Yet it is evidently not so. People are richer than ever, yet contentment and a sense of purpose seem to be conspicuous by their absence, and the process of secularisation which has accompanied increasing affluence does not seem to be resulting in any kind of personal or social utopia.

It has even been suggested (by the writer of an article[1] which appeared in Readers' Digest) that

> if Hollywood actors have a role to play, it is to teach us that happiness has nothing to do with fun. These rich, beautiful individuals have constant access to glamorous parties, fancy cars, expensive homes, everything that spells 'happiness'. But in memoir after memoir, celebrities reveal the unhappiness beneath all their fun: depression, alcoholism, drug addiction, broken marriages, troubled children, profound loneliness.

These words are all the more interesting because they are not part of some evangelistic address; the writer may or may not have been a Christian, but this was his simple reflection on life, without drawing any 'religious' conclusions. Despite all such experiences, however, he suggests:

> People continue to believe that the next, more glamorous party, more expensive car, more luxurious vacation, fancier home will do what all the other parties, cars, vacations, homes have not been able to do.

The same magazine once carried an advert which said:

> It will reassure you when you need it. It will help restore your confidence should it ever desert you. It will soothe and solace you after a hectic day. It will insulate you from the noise and chaos of the outside world. It will rebuild your morale, your ambitions. But most of all, it will remind you that your life has not been totally without success.

What was it that was being described with such fervent evangelistic zeal? It was an advertisement for Jaguar cars!

Despite all evidence to the contrary, people still present increasing affluence as the way to happiness and satisfaction.

In chapter 5 we suggested that life lacks meaning unless and until it is lived in relation to the God who created everything, and who, Christians believe, has acted for the salvation of a world in which there is so much trouble, discord, gloom and sin. In this chapter, we take up another challenge which Christianity puts to the world: apart from

God and his revelation, what basis can there be for morality?

The case of an American chat-show host, who was well-known for his liberal views on abortion, encapsulates this issue. He had no sympathy with the pro-life position, and he would even refuse to accept calls from men, because, he said, the issue has nothing to do with men. He read a newspaper article about the training regime of some female athletes in eastern Europe who were preparing for a competition. In this article it was explained that, as part of their muscle development programme, these girls would plan to become pregnant two or three months before a key race, reap the benefit of the enlarged muscle capacity experienced during the first two months of pregnancy and then abort the baby a few days before the race.

When the chat-show host read about this, he was horrified, and he unsparingly denounced such a practice. However, as Ravi Zacharias says in reporting the incident, 'He never explained his own inconsistency.'[2]

I suppose that most people would agree that such a practice is morally unacceptable, but our question here is: on what basis? *Why*, on the presenter's own pre-suppositions, was it so wrong? Where do you draw the line? These questions relate not only to the issue of abortion in particular, but to morality in general, and the need for some kind of basis for morality.

A biblical picture

In the Old Testament book of Jeremiah, we find these words from God: 'My people have committed two sins; they have forsaken me, the spring of living water, and have dug their own cisterns, broken cisterns that cannot hold water' (Jer.

2:13). There were two sources of water in these days: springs and cisterns, the latter being tanks in the ground, which were designed to retain any available water, but they were obviously second-best to spring water. One observer has written of these cisterns:

> The best cisterns, even those in solid rock, are strangely liable to crack, and are a most unreliable source of water; and if by constant care they are made to hold, yet the water has the colour of weak soap-suds, the taste of the earth or stable, is full of worms, and in the hour of greatest need it utterly fails.[3]

Anyone who had the choice between the two would always choose spring water. Anyone who had that choice – spring water or cistern water – and actually *chose* cistern water would be regarded as very odd; we would say to such a person, 'Why settle for that mucky water from the cistern when you could come to the spring and obtain fresh water?'

Jeremiah believed that *God* is the source of living water, and yet he saw what he regarded as the tragedy of people refusing that clear water and instead choosing to resort to their own cisterns, which turned out to be useless.

And we are suggesting that this is God's message through Jeremiah for today too. Jeremiah 2:19 says, 'Consider then and realise how evil and bitter it is for you when you forsake the Lord your God and have no awe of me, declares the Lord'; the emphasis falls on the words, 'for you'. Their rebellion was not only an affront to the holiness of God and disobedience to him; they were hurting themselves when they ignored and rebelled against God.

The same point was made in a detail from the story of Paul's conversion, when he heard the voice of God challenging him, 'Why are you kicking against the goads?' (Acts 26:14) – like a rebellious ox which kicks back against the spikes on the front of the cart and only hurts itself in the process.

Moral confusion

The Bible's message is that faith in God is the thing that brings real life, meaning and a basis for living, whereas the rejection of God and his ways brings frustration, meaninglessness and moral confusion. It is especially the last that we are concerned with here.

In the Old Testament book of Judges, there is described a time when people did what was right in their own eyes (Judg. 21:25). They made their own value judgements and decisions, without regard to anything which might be called an objective standard. The result, as described in that book, was moral and social chaos.

But our modern world is one in which people like to choose their own morality. It is not simply a question of whether people accept certain moral standards as binding on them – people always have to make their own choices on such matters. But there is a prevailing attitude of choosing one's own moral standards. This 'pick 'n' mix' approach to morality is reflected in the cartoon in a book by Graham Cray which depicts a man hammering together several boards to make a box – his personal morality. The slogans visible on the sides of the box say, 'Love others', 'Fiddle tax', 'Save the whales'.[4]

But is life liveable in a society where people simply choose their own values and combine them in any way they see fit?

It is obvious that many people today have thrown off 'religion' as a base for morality, relying rather on this personal choice than on any 'commands' from without.

Our assertion is that they are rather like car drivers who complained about the painted lines in a car park; they said, 'Why should we have to park where someone else tells us to park? Why shouldn't we be free to park wherever we like?' So they parked anywhere they liked. And what was the result? Chaos! Perhaps these car drivers would end up pleading with the authorities to give them back the old markings, because they managed better when there were guide-lines.

The Christian claim, unpalatable as it may be to many, and unpleasant as it may be to face up to, is that there *will be* chaos if people reject or neglect the moral principles which God has given us.

Understanding The Times refers to what it calls the bankruptcy of modern secularism. This much-vaunted secularism, reflected and pushed by the modern media, was supposed to bring freedom, happiness and contentment, but it has signally failed to 'deliver the goods'. The widespread departure from the standards and values associated with Christianity has not ushered in a wonderfully blissful and 'free' world.

One of the finest analysts of this 'bankruptcy of secularism' was Francis Schaeffer, who was described by Michael Green as, 'One of the most accomplished apologists of the middle of the twentieth century'.

Green says that Schaeffer 'asked far more questions than he gave answers. He was always trying to discover what the basic presuppositions were of the person to whom he was talking; and he would then drive that person relentlessly towards the logical conclusions of his presuppositions.'[5] For instance, when he was arguing with a young man who advocated the virtues of free sex, Schaeffer's immediate response was to ask for the name and phone number of his live-in girlfriend! 'The young man was furious, until he realised that he was hoist with his own petard.' On his own presuppositions, what was he protesting about?

On another occasion, he was debating with an anarchist who believed in using violence if that was needed. Schaeffer got some friends to hold the man down, picked up a cudgel and asked why, on the basis of the anarchist's own arguments, he shouldn't proceed to beat his brains to pulp. This is not the kind of behaviour one might anticipate from an evangelist, but he made his point. He was putting his finger on questions, which we said in the last chapter many people would rather leave unasked or ignored. Yet such issues need to be faced

Where can we find a basis for moral values? At the time of writing, there seems to be a renewed realisation that we do in fact need some kind of moral backbone in society. This has been brought to the fore by tragic events like the Dunblane massacre, by many instances of child abuse and by many other evidences of social disorder. Whether this current concern will bear fruit (rather than being simply a politically correct, or plainly political point) remains to be seen, for there have been other times when it seemed as if people recognised the need for moral foundations (such as the time of national soul-searching after the murder of young James Bulger) but the concern seemed to fade with the passage of time. Perhaps this is simply because people have not found a real basis *for* morality. Attention is easily diverted elsewhere; a devastating recent comment in *Punch* claimed that in recent times

Hollywood's excesses have rivalled those of ancient Rome, when the last emperors were forced to plumb the depths of sensation, cruelty and sadistic spectacle to keep the audiences at the Coliseum satisfied and, to a large extent, quiescent.[6]

'I'd like an argument please' is the title of an article which asks some significant and perhaps uncomfortable questions about the basis for morality. The argument is worth quoting at length:

[I]n a discussion where someone is arguing for the acceptance of pornography, you might start by saying: 'That's interesting. You think that pornography isn't such a bad thing – what reasons have you got for saying that?'

You don't want to be drawn into approving of pornography (or of censorship for that matter), but by asking your friends to give a reasoned defence of their position the focus immediately shifts onto the illogical basis of their view. Now, as they appeal to utility, it is your turn to call into question the long-term effects of pornography. How can they possibly know?

If they insist that free access to pornography will actually reduce sex crimes, you can push it one step further: 'What makes you think that reducing sex crimes is a good thing?' At this point you need to muster your courage, for you know in your bones that sex crimes are appalling. However, in the context of the argument, you are merely taking your opponent's view to its logical conclusion in order to expose its weakness and ultimate failure. He also knows in his bones that sex crimes are appalling, but he is now put in the position of having to defend his intuitive morality.

Of course, there is no defence for intuition if God has not created the world, and so your friend is left to flounder with arguments like: 'Where would the world be...?' and 'It's self-evident that everyone should be treated fairly' and 'Would you like to be treated like that?' These are the arguments of desperation. Morality has been reduced to pragmatism and personal opinion. You can conclude that his version of morality seems little more than: 'What I like is good and what I don't like is bad.'[7]

The writer also makes the point that the person who is not a Christian is in fact, whether he thinks about it or not, living on the capital of many generations of Christian teaching and influence: 'He has imbibed God's values without knowing it.' But when people throw off the foundational beliefs on which these values are built, they find the edifice of morality collapsing around them.

Belief and behaviour

Of course, it might be said against this line of thought that there are many good-living people who are unbelievers; Christians cannot claim a monopoly on goodness. In chapter 8 we will be considering the charge that it's Christians who put many people off Christianity, and we will have to plead guilty to the charge that Christians have often signally failed to live up to the standards of Christ. We will be making the point that the failure was that of Christians, not Christ; Jesus himself would not have condoned many of the things which have been done in his name. But it is undeniably true that many non-Christians have been decent, good-living people. It could even be said that some people without any professed allegiance to Christ sometimes put to shame the lives of others who do claim to be Christians.

As long ago as 1942, John Baillie wrote:

> Within the modern humanistic era there have been many shining examples of men who had given up all belief in God and were nevertheless filled with a zeal for righteousness, and a love for neighbour, which might put many Christians to shame. [But] it would appear that this is likely to be no more than a very temporary phenomenon. It cannot last long, and it may be that it has already largely passed away.[8]

And what has happened in the half century since these words were written?

Certainly, there is still a great deal of goodness in society and in many people – yet there can be no denying the fact that crime, immoral behaviour and social disintegration have increased.

To take just a few symptoms of this disintegration:

- Britain has the highest divorce rate in Europe, and whatever might be said about people not being forced to live out a sham, it is also sadly true that there has been a great increase in the amount of unhappiness and in the number of children deprived of stability in their formative years.

- It is not so long since murder was a front-page banner-headline event, whereas now it is tragically commonplace.

- Sport has been marred by violence.

- Politics has been tainted by sleaze.

- Television has been infected with so much that is sick, cynical or suggestive.

- Alcoholism and drug addiction ruin many lives.

- Aids raises many questions about our much-vaunted sexual revolution.

Of course there is a great deal of kindness and compassion around – thank God. Sometimes people complain about the fact that only bad things are reported by the media. Many newspapers, for instance, seem to be much more interested in stories about criminal and immoral behaviour than in stories about people acting generously or caringly; some go to great lengths to dig up gossip and to highlight scandals. Besides challenging such attitudes, we may take some comfort from the fact that it is wicked things that grab the headlines, for it would be a sad state of affairs if goodness and love were so uncommon that they were thought to be sensational and needed to be reported.

There is indeed much goodness, but it might well be argued that the consequences of unbelief are largely hidden in our society by the effects of many generations of Christian influence.

Jung Chan, the author of the best-selling book, *Wild Swans*, has expressed the point very starkly: 'If you have no god, no absolute power to answer to, then your moral code is that of society. If society is turned upside down, so is your moral code.'[9]

Of course this view – that there is a connection between loss of faith and moral confusion – is rejected by many people. The writer of a letter to The Herald (13.6.95) took

issue with claims which had been made that if Christian
doctrines are rejected, Christian ethics are sure to follow:

> The doctrines have indeed almost gone and many people
> who profess to believe in them actually seem to believe in a
> version of them that is so diluted as to be nugatory. None
> the less most people behave as well as they always did and
> in many ways ethical concerns have rarely been stronger.

Our response to such a statement must be one of
thankfulness that so many people do indeed act in a 'good'
and caring way, but we might also be tempted to say to the
writer of that letter: tell that to the many victims of violence
today, people who have suffered unprovoked attacks, or
who mourn the loss of loved ones brutally murdered; tell it
to the people who bear the scars of physical, sexual or
mental abuse. The 'ethical concerns [which] have rarely
been stronger' can sometimes be very selective concerns.
Environmentalism, for example, is a very fashionable
concern today, and obviously Christians (believing in the
Creator) should be entirely supportive of all efforts to
safeguard the natural world. But what about other moral
concerns, relating to honesty, practical love and plain
neighbourliness (Luke 10:36f.), sexuality, respect for life,
etc.?

The claim that people 'behave as well as they always
did' is hard to take seriously, and one may well think that
such complacent views are expressed either by people who
have a vested interest in justifying their atheistic secularism
or by people who have their heads in the sand. Certainly,
we should be very thankful for the vast amount of good that
exists in our society, but there is plenty of cause for concern
about the moral state of our nation today, and the Christian

claim is that there is a connection between widespread departure from Christian beliefs and an increasingly selfish, greedy, 'Look after number one' attitude and lifestyle.

Friedrich Nietzsche is regarded by many as one of the most influential philosophers of all time. It has been suggested that Adolf Hitler 'took Nietzsche's logic and drove the atheistic world view to its legitimate conclusion'. Following Nietzsche's own assertion that because God had died in the nineteenth century, the twentieth century would be the bloodiest century in human history, Hitler 'provoked the bloodiest, most unnecessary, most disruptive war in history'.[10]

Nietzsche himself had no time for the notion that we can reject God and still hang on to Christian morality. In 1888 he wrote in *Twilight of the Gods:*

> When one gives up Christian belief, one thereby deprives oneself of the right to Christian morality.... Christianity is a system, a consistently thought out and complete view of things. If one breaks out of it a fundamental idea, the belief in God, one thereby breaks the whole thing to pieces; one has nothing of any consequence left in one's hands.[11]

In quoting these words, Will Storrar refers also to the writer Chris Grieve (pen name 'Hugh MacDiarmid'):

> While many of his contemporaries in early twentieth century Scotland believed with Thomas Carlyle that they had thrown away only the husk of Biblical religion, belief in Jehovah, while keeping its kernel, belief in the high moral view of human life, Chris Grieve would have none of it; he had no time for the notion 'that you could destroy

the whole basis of the Christian religion and yet retain a few of its ethical principles'.[12]

Our greatest need

Secularisation was mentioned in some of the Presbyteries' returns as a barrier to belief, a kind of cultural ethos which tends to keep people away from Christianity. The secularism of today shows up our crying need for a better basis for living. We have considered the areas of meaning and morality, and seen that in both areas we experience chaos rather than contentment if we reject Christ. Our great need is for something to restore the guide-lines and give us a basis for morality. It is highly questionable whether we can have Christian virtues without the Christian beliefs that underlie them.

> Appreciation of the humanitarian Christian virtues is like the enjoyment of the fruits which have been cut off from the living tree. Cut freshly, these fruits are still infused with something of the original life from which they came. Preserved through time on the ice of habit, discipline, moral education, they may keep some of their flavour, though icy. But sooner or later, the fruit withers, and we have to return to the living tree for more.[13]

Are we not in a situation today where we need to return to that living tree? The Bible says that the 'fruit of the Spirit is love, joy, peace, patience, kindness, goodness, faithfulness, gentleness and self-control' (Gal. 5:22f.), and are not these the very qualities which are desperately needed nowadays? Paul describes them as the fruit *of the Spirit*; he was in no doubt that that is where they come from – from the effect of the Spirit of Jesus Christ in the hearts of those who give themselves to him in faith and commitment. No doubt he had Jesus' words in mind: 'By their fruit you will recognise them. Do people pick grapes from thornbushes, or figs from thistles? Likewise every good tree bears good fruit, but a bad tree bears bad fruit. A good tree cannot bear bad fruit, and a bad tree cannot bear good fruit' (Matt. 7:16-19).

Trees bear good fruit when they are well rooted and well nourished. The 'good tree' is one that has its roots firmly bedded in the soil. It draws nourishment from the ground, which in turn enables it to bear fruit.

This has been vividly illustrated from the devastation caused across the south-east of England in October 1987 by hurricane-force winds. For about three hours, winds of over one hundred miles per hour battered that area and destroyed an estimated sixteen million trees. The significant thing is that the hurricane followed four years of comparative drought which had resulted in the roots being very dry. This weakened grip made the trees vulnerable when the storm struck.

After describing this happening, Clifford Hill draws the parallel:

> For many years the faith of the nation has been in decline with the decrease in church attendance, the increase of secularism and the impact of other religions. The foundational beliefs of the nation have not been fed and watered. As the winds of change have begun blowing ever more strongly across the nation, the fate of the sixteen million trees may be taken as a symbol of the disaster that lies ahead unless there is a dramatic change – a slowing down of the rate of change, a re-emphasis upon

fundamental social values and a rebuilding of secure foundations to undergird the life of the nation.[14]

In Matthew 7, Jesus followed his words about the fruitful tree with a change of picture:

> Everyone who hears these words of mine and puts them into practice is like a wise man who built his house on the rock. The rain came down, the streams rose, and the winds blew and beat against that house; yet it did not fall, because it had its foundation on the rock. But everyone who hears these words of mine and does not put them into practice is like a foolish man who built his house on sand. The rain came down, the streams rose, and the winds blew and beat against that house, and it fell with a great crash. (Matt. 7:24-27)

His great challenge to us, both as individuals and as a society, is to consider the foundations on which we are building.

Notes

1.   Dennis Prager 'The Key to Lasting Happiness' condensed from Redbook, New York, 1989.
2.   R. Zacharias, *A Shattered Visage* (Baker, Grand Rapids, Michigan, 1990), p.184.
3.   W. H. Thomson, Quoted by D. Kidner, *The Message of Jeremiah* (IVP, Leicester, 1987), p.32.
4.   G. Cray, *The Gospel and Tomorrow's Culture* (CPAS, Warwick, 1994), p.3.
5.   M. Green, *Evangelism Through the Local Church* (Hodder & Stoughton, London, 1990), p.133.
6.   N. Norman in *Punch*, 6 September 1996.
7.   'I'd like an argument please', *The Briefing* (St. Matthias Press) 158, pp.8f.

8.   J. Baillie, *Invitation to Pilgrimage* (Oxford University Press, 1942), p.46.
9.   Quoted in *Daily Telegraph*, 8 September 1995.
10. R. Zacharias, op. cit., pp.59-61.
11. Quoted by W. Storrar, *Scottish Identity* (Handsel Press, Edinburgh, 1990), p.181.
12. Ibid., p.181.
13. J. Baillie, op. cit., p.47.
14. Clifford Hill, *Shaking The Nations* (Kingsway, Eastbourne, 1995), p.51.

Chapter 7

Eternity in Our Hearts?

In the last two chapters, we have been considering the barrier to Christianity which is presented by the secularism of today. In our secularised society, many have no knowledge of Christianity, many have no interest in it, and many feel no need of it.

New spirituality?

However, there seem also to be some signs today of a realisation of the barrenness of a purely materialistic and unspiritual attitude to life, and a number of people detect a new kind of spiritual search on the part of some.

In his foreword to the report on the Scottish church attendance census of 1994, Sir David McNee refers to secularisation as one of the primary causes of the churches' diminishing influence, but then he goes on:

> Today, as the 20th century draws to its close, a new mood is gaining ground. People are beginning to doubt a purely secular view of reality, suspicious that there is more than one dimension to the universe. Millions are setting out on a spiritual quest in search of ultimate reality.[1]

He then goes on to point out that many people are presently seeking to satisfy this need through oriental mysticism, New Age therapy and ancient pagan ritual.

John Drane offers a similar analysis.[2] He gives a fascinating quotation from the actress Joanna Lumley, who has said, 'We have gone through a very non-spiritual time this century', and who predicted: 'In the 1990s we're going to start finding our souls again.'

The problem (from a Christian point of view) is that so many people look elsewhere than to the gospel of Jesus Christ. In France, for example, which would be reckoned by many to be a strongly Roman Catholic country, there are said to be 26,000 priests but there are 40,000 professional astrologers registered for tax purposes!

Drane summarises:

> a dazzling and bewildering array of different spiritualities compete for attention, each of them claiming to be able to offer something that will help us to find our souls again, and chart a safe course for the future. The goods on offer in this religious market-place range from messages from spirit guides and extraterrestrials, to neo-paganism, celtic mythology and aboriginal spirituality – not to mention renewed interest in astrology and a vast range of psychological therapies offering the prospect of a renewed, holistic humanity.[3]

Your agreement or disagreement with this analysis will clearly depend on the particular people with whom you mix. No doubt there are many who do not fit into the picture painted above – people for whom the barrenness of materialism does not seem to be evident, or at least is making no difference. But it may be that there are indeed more people who are aware of the barrenness of a purely secular outlook than there have been for some time.

Unfortunately many people have given up the idea of a search *for truth*. Instead, they are looking for something that works in their life, and, whether it comes from Christianity, Buddhism or so-called paganism, all that matters is whether it seems to them to 'work'.

The Times reported on 16 August 1994 on the decision of the W. H. Smith organisation to introduce a 'personal development' section in five hundred bookshops in the United Kingdom. The report reflected on this decision:

> Without doubt there is a sudden international hankering for the spiritual and mystical. But why? There is no parallel return to organised religion. The trend is much more DIY, and the faith expected of readers is of an undemanding, semi-committed nature, without the effort required of mainstream church life. Nor do most of these books have a dark side; Satan and the wages of sin tend to go unmentioned. Welcome to the saccharin universe of New Age theology.

One of the responses to the *Barriers to Belief* survey (from the Presbytery of Inverness) observed, 'There is a considerable reservoir of faith to be tapped', but *Understanding The Times* makes the point that the Church may increasingly need to show why it believes that faith should be Christian faith.[4]

There is a great need for Christians to be equipped to give a reason for the hope they have within them (1 Pet. 3:15) and to give answers to the kind of objections to Christian belief which we are considering in this book.

A biblical 'critique of secularism'

Within the Bible there is one particular book which relates very interestingly to these themes. It is a book which was described by Professor G. S. Hendry as 'a critique of secularism and of secularised religion'.[5] It is the book of Ecclesiastes.

The eleventh verse of its third chapter says, 'God has set eternity in the hearts of men.' This comes in a well-known passage which has a fourteen-point over-view of the many and varied experiences of life (a time to be born and a time to die, a time to plant and a time to uproot, and so on), and always the question of the book is: what's the meaning of it all? Through all these changing scenes of life, is there some meaning, is there some grand design being worked out, do our lives have any real significance?

The book's refrain is well-known: 'Vanity of vanities; all is vanity.' That, it says, is life without God. It explores various possible sources of fulfilment and satisfaction, but they are all found wanting. That recurring refrain is not the author's own verdict upon life; he is rather seeking to highlight the illusory hopes which people entertain, and he does so with a view to introducing them to the real life which is to be found, he believes, through faith in and allegiance to the living God.

The Bible claims that, since this is so, people simply will not find fulfilment and meaning and a sense of purpose apart from him.

The New International Version Study Bible says about verse 11 ('He has made everything beautiful in its time'): 'God's beautiful but tantalising world is too big for us, yet its satisfactions are too small. Since we were made for eternity, the things of time cannot fully and permanently satisfy.'

God has set eternity in our hearts, and because that is so, people will never be satisfied with any amount of goods or pleasures of this world.

Many famous testimonies to this truth could be adduced:

The actor, Larry Hagman, most famous for his role as J. R. Ewing of 'Dallas', said, 'I have a lot of money, but there still seems a void in my life.'

Boris Becker achieved great success in tennis, but came close to taking his own life because of a sense of emptiness and meaninglessness:

> I had won Wimbledon twice before, once as the youngest player. I was rich. I had all the material possessions I needed: money, cars, women, everything.... I know that this is a cliché. It's the old song of the movie and pop stars who commit suicide. They have everything, and yet they are so unhappy.... I had no inner peace.[6]

And the film-star, Errol Flynn, wrote in *My Wicked, Wicked Ways*:

> There I was, sitting on top of the world. I had wealth, friends, I was internationally known, I was sought after by women. I could have anything money could buy. Yet I found that at the top of the world there was nothing. I was sitting on a pinnacle, with no mountain under me.[7]

These (and many other) testimonies speak of the reality of this stubborn truth – that God has set eternity in our hearts, and our lives will always be incomplete without him. Ecclesiastes ruthlessly drives home the point in verse 19 of Chapter 3: 'Everything is meaningless. All go to the same place; all come from dust, and to dust all return. Who knows if the spirit of man rises upward?'

Without God, it *is* all meaningless and futile, and, painful though it may be, people need to be led to face up to the logic of their own beliefs or lack of beliefs, to see where their attitudes lead.

According to John's account of the gospel story, there was a time when many followers of Jesus fell away, and Jesus addressed the twelve: 'You do not want to leave me too, do you?' Peter was the one who spoke up; he said, 'Lord, to whom shall we go? You have the words of eternal life' (John 6:66ff.). Peter had somehow come to see that Jesus' way was the way that made sense; there really wasn't any other way.

The demands of Christianity

But many of those who were held back from following him were perhaps held back by the sheer fact that Christ's way is demanding. Matthew 19, for example, tells of a man who approached Jesus with the question, 'What good thing must I do to get eternal life?' He was a man who seemed to have everything going for him. He was rich, he was still young and he was a man of some influence. Yet he was aware that his religion lacked something; he hadn't yet found satisfaction and the assurance of eternal life.

However, what happened was that Jesus put his finger on this man's idol, namely his money and possessions. Jesus told him that his possessions were the barrier in his way, and he needed to get rid of them, and then come and follow Jesus. And the story tells us, 'When the young man heard this, he went away sad, because he had great wealth.' He wasn't prepared to pay the cost. He wanted to be a Christian, but he didn't want it that much!

It is often pointed out also that Jesus let him go. He did not call back this potential convert to re-negotiate a better 'deal' for him.

Others may have been held back also because they weren't prepared to pay the cost of following Christ. Jesus was up-front in his emphasis on the demands of discipleship; he did not try to attract followers by suggesting that it would be easy to follow him.

Perhaps there are many today too, for whom a major barrier is the demand of Christ, the changes which would have to be made if they were to be serious about following Christ.

This is not a barrier to belief which was mentioned by those non-believers who were approached in the survey, but then it is perhaps unlikely that they would mention it. And, without minimising the other barriers which we are considering in this book, we may suspect that many people are indeed held back by the knowledge that Christianity, if taken seriously, makes considerable demands on a person's life.

In this connection it is interesting to reflect on some further words of Sir Thomas Taylor:

[T]hose who take the Bible seriously know that where the God of the Bible is concerned, men search for Him in precisely the way that the average mouse searches for the average cat.[8]

We have spoken about a considerable degree of spiritual search today, but Taylor said, 'where *the God of the Bible* is concerned...'. This bears out what has been said about the way in which people seek to satisfy this spiritual longing in their hearts by resorting to other, less demanding, religions or systems.

It is all very well, as C. S. Lewis put it, to 'dabble in religion' (see chapter 1, page 6), but we aren't sure that we want it to go further than that. God has 'planted eternity in our hearts', but so many people attempt to satisfy this hunger with something else, something more congenial, something less demanding. The God of the Bible is not an undemanding patron-saint. Of course Christianity claims to be good news of all that God has done and wants to do in our lives, but it is also a message from one who wants to bring our lives into conformity with his will. It is only in him that we can find the real fulfilment of our human destiny, but commitment to him makes demands on us.

Could it be that some of the popularity of other forms of spirituality (New Age or whatever) arises from the fact that they do not make very great demands; people can pursue them, even if they want to be left alone to live their lives as they want to live them, whereas genuine commitment to Jesus Christ is bound to make a difference to people's lives.

It is because God has 'set eternity in the hearts of men' that life 'works' when we live it his way. He invites us to 'taste and see that the Lord is good' (Psalm 34:8); he invites us to find fullness of life (John 10:10) in him.

Peer pressure

One other barrier to belief might be mentioned before closing this chapter, and that is 'peer pressure'. Many people seem to be held back from Christianity by the fear of what others would think of them, say about them or even do to them. Among young people especially, it is not reckoned to be 'cool' to be religious, and some are put off by that.

One of the oldest members of my congregation told me about how, 70 years ago, he found other young men laughing at those of them who went to church, so this is no new thing. Maybe it has always been part of the Christian challenge.

It was recognised as such by a teenager mentioned in a report[9] of a Scripture Union camp; he had learned about Christ and was seriously considering Christian commitment, but, as the leader reported,

> Before parting, one of the lads said to me, 'How will I tell my mammy an' ma pals I want tae be a Christian? I'll get slagged rotten.'

This is a very real factor for many, and perhaps the only thing that can be said to people who are affected by it would be: is your response to the message of Christ so *un*important that you should be put off by the attitude of others, or isn't this something that calls for faith and commitment, whatever others may say about it? It may be that other people will give more respect than is expected to those who take a stand and seek to live sincere and consistent lives, but even if they do not, the attitude of other people is a very poor criterion on which to make a decision of such importance.

John Newton experienced a very radical change in his life. He had been a wild-living, foul-mouthed slave-ship captain, but then the grace of God broke into his life, and one of the things he later wrote was:

Saviour, if of Zion's city
I, through grace, a member am,
Let the world deride or pity,
I will glory in thy name.[10]

When our survey found that many adults too seemed to be 'pressurised by the prevailing apathy and indifference about Christianity'; when it posed the question as to whether there might not even be a certain political correctness in some quarters about alleging that the Church is boring and Christianity irrelevant; when it concluded that 'It takes considerable courage to deviate from the accepted norm' – it confirmed that the call is there for a response that is unhindered by anything other people may think or say or do.

John Drane claims:

> The fact is that allegedly 'secular' people are far more religious than for many generations. Twenty years ago, being religious was often seen as a sign of weakness, or even psychological deficiency. Now, it's almost avant garde to be engaged in this spiritual search. That search might easily encompass all manner of seemingly bizarre and incredible beliefs and practices, but it is unlikely to have a place for whatever the Church has to offer.[11]

This book, in seeking to respond to people's barriers to faith, is an attempt to encourage the sceptic to take another look. G. K. Chesterton famously said that 'Christianity has not so much been tried and found wanting as found difficult and left untried.'[12]

Notes

1. *Prospects For Scotland* (National Bible Society of Scotland, Edinburgh, 1995), p.iii.
2. J. Drane, *Evangelism for a New Age* (Marshall Pickering, London, 1994), p.14.
3. Ibid., p.16.
4. *Understanding The Times* (Saint Andrew Press, Edinburgh, 1995), p.8.
5. *New Bible Commentary* (InterVarsity Fellowship, London, 1953), p.538.
6. Quoted in Alister McGrath and Michael Green, *Springboard for Faith* (Hodder & Stoughton, London, 1993), p. 65.
7. Quoted in a printed sermon by Michael Perrott in *The Christian Herald,* 20 August 1983.
8. T. Taylor, *Where One Man Stands* (Saint Andrew Press, Edinburgh, 1960), p.84.
9. Fred Whitnall, in *Steeple News,* magazine of The Steeple Church, Dundee (June 1995), p.6.
10. 'Glorious Things of Thee are Spoken', *Revised Church Hymnary* (Oxford University Press, Glasgow, 1929), no. 206.
11. J. Drane, op. cit., p.184.
12. G. K. Chesterton, *What's Wrong with the World?* (Cassell & Co., London, 1910), p.17.

Chapter 8

'It's the Church that Puts Me Off!'

It has been wryly asserted that the church must be in God's hands because, seeing the people who have run it, it couldn't possibly have gone on existing if there hadn't been some help from above!

This tongue-in-cheek statement gives a round-about answer to one of the strongest arguments against Christianity, namely the allegation that the faults and failings of the Christian church make it impossible to believe.

It was stated succinctly by a New Age writer who made the terse comment, 'Christianity has not been very Christian.'[1] Any enquiry into the issues which are seen as barriers to the acceptance of Christianity today (and possibly in any day) is liable to come up with the fact that many people are put off by the church.

In the 1993 Scottish survey, this issue of disenchantment with the church was indeed revealed as a major barrier to belief; 'The surveys also noted that there were those who said positive things about the Church, but it is undeniable that the criticisms are serious, sustained and widespread.'[2]

The Presbytery of Aberdeen, for example, said that it was remarkable how often the charge of hypocrisy was levelled at Christians, and a teenager somewhere in Wigtown and Stranraer expressed disgust at what he described as the astonishing amount of hypocrisy he had experienced in the church community as a whole (and he was still only in his teens!).

Other responses referred to the failure of church members to live up to their ideals, the failure of some particular minister, and well-publicised expressions of doubt on the part of church leaders about this or that aspect of traditional Christian teaching.

Some people refer to the church's representatives and the alleged hypocrisy of their lives, some to the church's history and the dreadful things which have been done in the past in the name of religion, and others to the church's allegedly boring services. People say, 'Look at all the wars which have been fought in the name of religion', and, 'Look at the way religion has been used to prop up various vested interests and keep down certain classes of people.' And we have to admit that the history of the church has been darkened by things like the acceptance for so long of the institution of slavery, by the Inquisition, by the kind of Christianity that sought to give a theological justification for something as anti-Christian as apartheid. Someone challenged me along these lines about a newspaper report she had read about a church somewhere where the leaders decided that its doors would have to be kept locked – not because of problems of vandalism or theft, but because homeless people were finding shelter there!

And this point arises in connection with a church which claims to be based on a book which has no time for 'theoretical' religion divorced from the actualities of life. J. B. Phillips paraphrased God's message in Amos 5:21-24:

I loathe and despise your festivals; your meetings for sacrifice give me no pleasure. You may bring me your burnt-offerings, your meal-offerings, or your thank-offerings of fat cattle, and I shall not so much as look at them. Let me have no more of your noisy hymns. My ears are closed to the music of your harps. Instead, let justice roll on like a mighty river, and integrity like a never-failing stream!

So much for faith without works, worship without practical service, private devotions without loving compassion for needy people.

The point may be summed up by the story with which Stephen Gaukroger begins his chapter, 'What about all the hypocrites?' He tells of:

a recent Wednesday night meeting at our church [when] I asked people to list the reasons why they felt Christianity was unpopular with the people they worked with. There were over a hundred people at the meeting from a wide variety of backgrounds and occupations. Lots of reasons were given but the most frequently mentioned was the behaviour of Christians. The thrust of the attack was – 'Christianity is great, it's Christians who are a pain in the neck.'[3]

This is not a very encouraging story for those who are in the church, but it sums up what many feel.

Is Christianity discredited by hypocritical Christians, by its bad record or by its boring services? We will leave the issue of the allegedly boring services till the next chapter, and consider here the past and present failings of those who have made up the church and who make it up now.

How do we face up to the assertion that disenchantment with Christians and the church is a barrier to belief?

Imperfect Christians

We begin with a frank admission. When people say that the church is made up of hypocrites, they are absolutely right! It's true; the church is made up entirely of human beings whose behaviour does not match up to their beliefs.

But then, the point is that *all* human beings are, to a greater or lesser extent, hypocrites (unless there are somewhere some people who are truly perfect specimens of goodness and morality). Nobody really lives up to his or her own highest ideals; there is always a gap between our ideals and the reality of our lives.

And if it's true that all human beings are, in this sense, hypocrites, then the church is bound to be made up of such hypocrites, and the only question will really be whether the gospel message is making any difference. Is the gospel producing people who are becoming less hypocritical than they were? That is the real issue.

In reply to the charge that the imperfections and even hypocrisies of professed Christians form a barrier to belief, we have to say: you must consider where a person has come *from*. This is a point Robert Burns made, from his own perspective, in one of his poems; he wanted to encourage a generous attitude to the failings of others, because, for one thing, no-one can tell what battles these others have fought to be where they are. He wrote:

> Then gently scan your brother Man,
> Still gentler sister Woman;
> Tho' they may gang a kennin wrang,

To step aside is human;
One point must still be greatly dark,
The moving *Why* they do it;
And just as lamely can ye mark,
How far perhaps they rue it.
Who made the heart, 'tis *He* alone
Decidedly can try us,
He knows each chord its various tone,
Each spring its various bias;
Then at the balance let's be mute,
We never can adjust it;
What's *done* we partly may compute,
But know not what's *resisted.* [4]

If you were inclined to make negative remarks of any kind about someone who smokes 20 cigarettes a day, it might alter your attitude somewhat if you learned that the person concerned, until very recently, smoked 30 a day. He still has a problem, but at least he's going in the right direction.

Similarly, Stephen Gaukroger gives the illustration of someone who claims to be a Christian but he steals paper-clips from his place of work. That's wrong – of course it is. But he goes on, 'if Joe had been a psychopathic killer, and now only takes paper-clips from work, I'd say a good case could be made out for the effectiveness of his Christianity'.[5] Fair point; that is no excuse for taking paper clips of course, but it puts the whole matter into a different perspective. Joe is on the right road, despite his faults; he is moving forward.

At the personal level, it means that if someone points to my far-from-perfect life, I can only admit my own failings and say, 'I may not be all I could be, but the question is whether I am any better than I would be if I were not a Christian.' The issue is not how far along the road of holiness I may be, but whether I am moving forward from where I used to be.

This has to be our response to this barrier to belief – to insist that the church is, after all, made up of ordinary people who do not claim to be perfect. It is the point Paul made in 2 Corinthians 4:7. He had no illusions about the make-up of the church, and he made no great claims for himself. None was more enthusiastic than he in extolling the glories of the gospel, the amazing wonder of the good news of God's grace in Jesus Christ and all that he has done for the world's salvation. But, so far as his own worth as a representative of that Lord was concerned, he described himself as 'the least of the apostles, not deserving to be called an apostle' (1 Cor. 15:9) and even as 'the worst of sinners' (1 Tim. 1:15).

In 2 Corinthians 4:7 he wrote, 'We have this treasure in jars of clay, to show that this all-surpassing power is from God and not from us.' A kind of contemporary version of the 'jars of clay' recently featured in a catalogue advertisement for a secure container for valuables. It was in the shape of a tin and looked like a tin of beans, the idea being that a burglar would hardly imagine that your most precious belongings were stored in a bean-tin.

In this verse, Paul refers to 'jars of clay', which do not look special or valuable, but they *contain* something precious and valuable. He's referring to the message of the gospel of Christ. That is the precious thing, while the 'jars of clay' stand for Paul himself and the other human bearers of the gospel. People shouldn't pay too much attention to the container, but rather to the precious contents. It is not that there is an intention to mislead (as with the device of the bean-tin), but the fact is that the wonderful message of the gospel always has been contained in such jars of clay.

This is the Bible's answer to people who say that the church has put them off Christianity. Christians do not claim to be perfect specimens of that Christianity that Jesus came to bring. Our attitude is: don't pay attention to the container but to that which is contained in it; don't concentrate on the church which seeks to serve Christ, but on the Christ whom the church seeks to serve.

The church's divisions

Before going on, we may pause to consider another of the failings identified by those who participated in the 1993 survey. Someone in Uist Presbytery said, 'As a non-believer, I find the vehemence of disagreements between different factions of the church difficult to understand.' People point to the cliques, factions and disunity which have sometimes marred the life of the church.

In Scotland, we have had Reformed Presbyterians and Associated Presbyterians, Original Secessionists and United Secessionists, Burghers and Anti-Burghers, Auld Lichts and New Lichts, United Presbyterians, Free Presbyterians, and so on, almost ad infinitum! Several points may be made on this issue.

One is that there may be no excuse for disunity, but at least we should remember that when we are talking about 'religious' issues, we are talking about issues on which people feel very deeply. It is not on a level with whether you are interested in football, fashion or philately. People may become passionately committed to such pastimes, but few even of the most enthusiastic devotees would claim that their interests are matters of life and death and that it is vitally important that other people come to share their enthusiasm. It doesn't really matter whether I support a particular football team, favour a particular style in fashion or put everything into stamp-collecting. But when it comes to the issues which lie at the heart of 'religion', we are talking about matters of the greatest importance. Christians believe that the questions involved in our response to Jesus Christ are crucial for everyone – both for their immediate fulfilment in this life and for their eternal wellbeing. Without for the present entering into the question of whether such a view is warranted, the very fact that Christians take such issues so seriously means that differences will not seem trivial but very important.

A second point is that most Christians, even if they disagree on some points, would regard the things which they have in common as more significant than the things on which they differ. In some churches people stand to pray, in others they sit and in still others they kneel; in some churches infants are baptised, while others baptise only adult believers; some Christians are pacifists while others are not. Yet most Christians would assert that what they share is far greater and more important than any of the things on which they differ.

And the third consideration is the passing remark that this proneness to division is possibly not so much a specifically Christian failing as a generally human one. Consider this statement by Robin Skynner and John Cleese: 'They're always splitting up and forming separate groups, which themselves split up after a time.'[6] 'They' in this sentence refers not to the church, but to the political groupings of our country. These writers go on to say: 'In the red corner, there is the Communist Party of Great Britain, the New Communist Party, the Vanguard Group, the Socialist Workers' Party (Trotskyist), the Socialist Party of Great Britain (Marxist), the International Marxist Group' –

and so on, listing no fewer than forty-four socialist groups. Then, on the other hand, complete with swastikas etc., we have the National Front, the British Movement, the Adolf Hitler Commando Group, the Racial Preservation Society, altogether twenty groupings. Without going into the authors' psychological explanation of this tendency, it is interesting that the Christian church is not the only body which seems to be prone to division.

However, even after all of that has been said, you might still expect more unity in the church than has actually characterised its life. The church is, after all, described as 'the body of Christ' (1 Cor. 12:27); it is meant to be giving visible expression to the ways of Christ – and Christ prayed that his people might be one. Christians need to take to heart the challenge about displaying the essential unity that comes from Christ, and even when they disagree on certain points, they need to learn to do so with courtesy, humility and tolerance.

As for the church's divisions being a barrier to faith, we come back to the point that Christ only has imperfect human beings to work with. The gospel is treasure, but it is contained in jars of clay – that is, ordinary, imperfect human beings.

The hospital, the building-site and the common cold

Several analogies may be pressed into service in drawing out this point.

a) The church is sometimes likened to a hospital. It would be a strange thing if someone observed the workings of a hospital for a time, and then complained, 'Can't be

much of a hospital, this; all the people here are sick or
injured'! You would say to such a person, 'Of course they
are – that's the kind of people for whom a hospital exists.'
Healthy people don't need a hospital. Hospitals are always
likely to be full of people who have something wrong.

The church is God's hospital; it is for people who realise
that there is something wrong with them in another way,
and who are indeed at various stages of being treated –
even for hypocrites who are being healed of their hypocrisy.
Just as you wouldn't expect a hospital to be filled with
people who are perfectly fit and healthy, so it's no use
expecting the church to be full of people who are spiritually
or morally perfect.

A hospital exists to help people get better in one sense,
and the church exists to help people by God's grace get
better in another sense.

b) Again, the church can be likened to a building-site.
What would you think of someone who went to a building-
site and started moaning about all the mess that could be
seen – heaps of bricks lying about, piles of timber, mud and
dirt and dust: 'there are cranes and JCBs and other vehicles
cluttering the place – doesn't look like much of a house to
me!' To such a person you might well say, 'But the job isn't
finished yet; there may be a bit of a mess now, but when the
work is finished, everything will be tidied up, and there
will be a fine new house, with everything spick and span.'

Again, that is like the Church of God: it is God's
building-site, and he isn't finished yet. Rome wasn't built in
a day, and neither is the Kingdom of God! It takes time for
the characters of the ordinary people who make up the
church to be changed into his likeness. Hopefully there will

be progress in this life, although it won't be until this life is over that the task will be complete.

c) Another analogy relates to the realm of health. Imagine someone taking out a handkerchief to clear his nose, and someone else saying to him, 'Do you have a cold?' He might reply, 'Well, I've *had* a cold; I was feeling really miserable but I'm getting better; it's just at the clearing-up stage.'

That too bears some analogy to the faults and failings of professed Christians: the actual underlying problem has been dealt with, but it's taking time for everything to clear up. Paul's words in Romans 7 relate to this subject. If anyone ever sought to live a godly and Christ-like life, it was Paul. (In Acts 24:16, for example, we find him saying, 'I strive always to keep my conscience clear before God and man.') Yet in Romans 7:15 we find his testimony: 'I do not understand what I do. For what I want to do I do not do, but what I hate I do.... I have the desire to do what is good, but I cannot carry it out. For what I do is not the good I want to do; no, the evil I do not want to do – that I keep on doing.' Here is the dilemma of an imperfect man who genuinely wants to live a good life.

These are some analogies which may help in answering the challenge that the church is a barrier to belief. The church is made up of people who do not claim to be perfect specimens of Christianity, but simply forgiven sinners who are seeking to make their own pilgrim's progress.

The positive side

However, there is something else that needs to be considered. If it is possible to point to the imperfections of professing Christians, there is another side of the coin. It is also true that the message of Christ has made an enormous difference for good in the lives of many people, and in the life of the world through those who have taken Christian discipleship seriously.

The Christian faith (or, as we believe, Christ himself) has been making an enormous difference for the better throughout these two millennia. This may not prove the truth of the Christian position, but it ought to be remembered in relation to this claim that so much wickedness has been perpetrated in the name of Christianity.

A chemist friend of mine is keen on emphasising the principle that care in sampling is at least as important as care in analysis. This principle, he says, was impressed upon him early in his career as an industrial chemist when he was involved in sampling dyes. It would not do for him to simply draw off some fluid from the top of a large drum and then subject it to analysis, because that sample might not be a typical sample of the whole. There may have been a settling of sediment, and great care needs to be taken in obtaining a suitable sample.

In the matter under consideration here, it is all too easy for the critics of Christianity to point to the poor lives of people who are 'supposed to be church members', without considering whether they are in fact looking at a fair sample. In one sense, there is only one point of sampling for Christianity, namely Christ himself, and we will come back to that, but even at this human level, we might plead with people not to judge Christianity by the worst examples they can find.

I once had a lawnmower which would have tried the patience of a saint! I would be ready to start the job, but the machine wouldn't be ready to start at all; many a day I almost dislocated my shoulder in pulling that draw-cord time after time. However, I did not conclude that there's no such thing as a decent lawnmower, and resort to purchasing a sheep instead. The problem lay with *that* lawnmower.

Similarly, if you invite me to listen to something on your radio and you switch it on and then find that the reception is poor and we can't make out what's being said, then I do not conclude that there is no such thing as radio and all your claims about sound being carried over the air-waves are delusions. If I drew such a conclusion, you would think I was being ridiculous; obviously the fault lies with this particular radio.

And the faults of a Christian prove not that there's something wrong with Christianity, but that there is something wrong with this particular Christian; he or she is, after all, only a 'jar of clay'.

Making a difference

This brings us back to our main answer to this charge that the hypocrisy of Christians is a barrier to belief. The question is that of whether the gospel of Christ is in fact resulting in people's lives being changed for the better. Michael Green was in no doubt that this is so. In his little paperback, 'Man Alive!', he discusses among other things the idea that the central belief of Christianity, namely the resurrection of Christ from the dead, came about as a result of a hallucination on the part of the disciples. He comments:

> This message of a risen Lord had a force for good which no hallucination has ever had. Through the risen Christ families were united after years of estrangement, immoral men became chaste and self-centred men became filled with love for others. Wherever it has gone, this gospel has changed the characters of those who received it, and it still does. Some hallucination![7]

They may be famous people who have made a great difference to the lives of their fellow human beings, or they may be people unknown to the world, but Christianity has certainly transformed the lives of very many people over the years. Perhaps you know someone like this – not a paragon of virtue or a 'saint' (in the popular sense of that word), but still, a person whose life and character is growing in Christ-likeness. This may not prove the truth or reality of the things which the person believes, but it is certainly evidence which deserves to be taken into account.

The prophet Ezekiel had a vision in which a stream of water was flowing out from the temple of God, a healing stream. He said, 'Where the river flows, everything will live' (Ezek. 47:9). Christians must repent of everything that has been unworthy in their history and in their own living, but we may also claim that it is historically true that Christianity has brought many blessings to humanity. Schools and hospitals owe their existence to the influence of Jesus Christ through his people, and many social improvements have been brought about through the same influence.

A Church of Scotland booklet published some years ago about the famous meeting between Dr David Livingstone, the explorer and missionary, and H. M. Stanley, the journalist, suggested:

> The meeting was of great significance... for it marked the end of one era in Afro-European relations and the opening of a new one. Livingstone was the last of the old line of men caring about Africa and seeking her development directly for the benefit of her people. Stanley, a brave man, but a traveller willing to shoot his way through if blocked by a chief (a thing Livingstone never once did) represented the new interest in Africa as an area for colonisation and for new raw materials to be developed for the benefit of Europe.[8]

To take an example from the other end of the social scale from Livingstone with his humble origins in Blantyre, we might think of the 7th Earl of Shaftesbury. He formed what was then known as the Ragged School Union and worked for the passing of various Acts of Parliament which improved living and working conditions for children and adults of Victorian times. The present-day Shaftesbury Society is one of the country's leading Christian social welfare charities. Again, one could refer to Dr Barnardo, William Wilberforce, Elizabeth Fry and General Booth. One thinks of Father Damien giving his life for the lepers and Martin Luther King giving his life for racial integration. One thinks of Tear Fund, or the caring work of a body such as the Church of Scotland's Board of Social Responsibility, with work that covers the vast spectrum of human need, expressing love and care in Jesus' name every day of life.

The fact that Christians have done much good does not prove the truth of their faith, nor would anyone claim that Christians have some kind of monopoly on compassion, but it needs to be remembered that all these sad and bad things which have been done in the name of Christianity do not give the whole picture. There is a positive side too.

Dr W. E. Sangster used to tell of his surprise at hearing of a tribe of moon-worshippers. He said he had heard of sun-worshippers, but was puzzled by the idea of worshipping the moon. When he asked about it, the explanation he received was that they didn't worship the sun because it shines in the day-time when there's plenty of light anyway, whereas the clever moon shines at night-time when it's dark and we're badly in need of all the light we can get! Sangster used the story to illustrate the fact that people are all the time living in the light of Christ, even if they don't realise it.

A transforming power

What has been true socially has also been true personally. It was so in the beginning. Paul was a realist so far as human nature is concerned, and in 1 Corinthians 6:9f. he wrote about the kind of people who would 'not inherit the kingdom of God': the sexually immoral, idolaters, adulterers, male prostitutes, homosexual offenders, thieves, the greedy, drunkards, slanderers, swindlers. It is an interesting – and challenging – list; but the following words speak volumes of the difference Christ was making in the real lives of real men and women in these days: 'and that is what some of you were'. Now, however, their lives had been transformed by the gospel of Christ.

This transformation has been repeated over and over again since then. For example, consider the fact that churches all over the world sing hymns which were written by John Newton. Once, such a thing would have been dismissed as a crazy and impossible idea – never in a lifetime of Sundays would John Newton become a hymn-writer; the name of Jesus Christ was nothing but an oath to him. Yet it was John Newton who wrote, 'How sweet the name of Jesus sounds in a believer's ear', along with many other hymns which are still commonly used, including 'Amazing Grace', his testimony to the change that had taken place in his own life and experience.

Another interesting testimony to this positive influence of Jesus Christ came unexpectedly from a man who himself had little time for Christianity. It is said that the French sceptic, Voltaire, refused to allow his friends to discuss atheism in front of the servants, because if it spread, morality would collapse. He said that he wanted his lawyer, his tailor, his valet, even his wife, to believe in God, because if they did, he would be robbed less and cheated less. This is an interesting comment. Presumably he thought they were all deluded, and that Christianity was merely 'useful' in certain ways, but perhaps his words give unconscious testimony to the reality of Christ's influence.

This, then, is one part of an answer to this assertion that the church's history is a barrier to belief. There have indeed been some dreadful things done in the name of Christianity, and we cannot deny it, but we can also remember and take account of the fact that Christianity's influence on the world has been enormously for the world's betterment.

Sometimes, of course, this betterment has seemed a long time coming. The question has often been posed, 'Why didn't the New Testament writers call slavery a wicked thing and demand its immediate abolition?' Surely it was always inconsistent with the teaching of Christ, and we would all regard such an institution as quite unacceptable. However, it is all very well to look at the matter from the vantage-point of our later situation; but the likelihood is that, if the New Testament writers had urged immediate action, it would probably have led to much bloodshed. It may have taken too long for the effects of the gospel of Christ to challenge this institution of slavery, but, 'At least he (Paul) helped to light the fuse of the time bomb which would eventually explode the whole system.'[9]

The issue of truth

In this chapter, we have considered two principles in answer to the charge that the past and present faults of Christians form a barrier to belief. The first is that the church is made up of ordinary, fallible human beings who do not claim to be perfect, but believe in the forgiving and renewing power of Christ. The other principle is that, although it is true that unworthy things have been done in the name of Christianity, it is also true that many Christians have helped greatly to make this world a better place.

The other principle – the main thing in all of this – is the insistence that people should judge Christianity not by Christians but by Christ. Good things done by Christians do not prove the truth of Christianity; neither do unworthy things done by Christians affect the issue of the truth or otherwise of Christianity.

It is certainly true that Christians are meant to be 'witnesses' for Jesus Christ, that he said, 'By their fruits you shall know them' (Matt. 7:16) and that we are failing 'if our light grows dim'. It is also true that the challenge for Christians is to take on board the criticisms that are made. There is the call for penitence over our failure properly to represent Christ, along with an endeavour to present a better witness to the world in his name. People have a right to say, 'Show me by your life that you are redeemed and then I will believe in your Redeemer.'

But still, Jesus did not say that his followers would be perfect, and the real challenge of Christianity is the challenge to respond to Christ and his person and message, not to the inadequate lives of his representatives.

In 2 Corinthians 4:5 Paul wrote, 'We do not preach ourselves but Jesus Christ as Lord, and ourselves as your servants for Jesus' sake.' That's all – just servants, who would point you to our Master.

The challenge of Christianity is not: how do you respond to the lives of those who profess to be Christians? It is rather: how do you respond to the claims of Christ on your heart and mind and soul? It is not, 'What do you think of the church?' but, 'What do you think of Christ?'

As an aside, it might be remarked that anyone who objects to hypocrisy is, to that extent, on Christ's side. He was very open in his rejection of hypocrisy; indeed some of his words must have caused large shock-waves in the minds of those who first heard them. He talked about people who honour God with their lips but whose hearts are far from him (Mark 7:6); he spoke critically of people who liked to appear clean on the outside, but were dirty within (Matt. 23:25); he even said, 'Woe to you, teachers of the law and Pharisees, you hypocrites! You are like whitewashed tombs, which look beautiful on the outside but on the inside are full of dead men's bones and everything unclean. In the same way, on the outside you appear to people as righteous but on the inside you are full of hypocrisy and wickedness' (Matt. 23:27-28). Let no-one suggest Jesus minced his words; let no-one suggest he courted popularity at any cost; let no-one suggest he was easy on hypocrisy.

Hypocrisy is no part of true Christianity. There is no question of trying to *defend* hypocrisy as if it were desirable or acceptable. In fact, real Christianity has no time for deliberate hypocrisy, and nobody who reads the New Testament could ever think it would have.

I say 'deliberate hypocrisy' intentionally, for this is a different thing from the *failure* of Christians to live up to Christian standards. Where there are people genuinely seeking, with God's help, to trust and obey Christ more fully, and yet they fall short and sometimes stumble and fall down, that is a different matter altogether from the situation in which people blatantly act on double standards, and make little or no attempt to live up to what they profess.

Church history has seen attempts to root out such hypocrisy, to create a so-called pure church, but even the original twelve disciples included Judas, and the apostle John could write about people who had been part of what we sometimes call the visible church, but they had gone out, because they were never really part of the true church (1 John 2:19).

However, real Christianity has no time for the deliberate hypocrisy that makes a Christian profession but makes no attempt to live a life that is consistent with that profession. That is our response to the challenge that disenchantment with the church presents a barrier to belief. The easily-identified failings of professing Christians do not discredit Christianity. As my incompetence on a golf course does not discredit golf, my shameful inadequacies in Christian living do not discredit Christianity either. Clearly, it is for all Christians to take on board all that is said about the church putting people off Christianity. After all, the Bible clearly says that Christians ought to be living exemplary lives. Jesus famously said to his disciples, 'You are the light of the world... let your light shine before men, that they may see your good deeds and praise your Father in heaven' (Matt. 5:14-16). In many other places the Bible asserts that the lives of Christians should remind people of Jesus, and there is a constant challenge to those who are Christians to live such lives that they do *not* put people off Christianity. The church must seek, with God's help, to put its own house in order.

But the main challenge to the critic is: consider Christ. The last chapter of John's gospel tells of an occasion when Peter referred to one of the other disciples and said, 'Lord, what about him?' Jesus' answer was, '*If* I want him to remain alive until I return what is that to you? You must follow me' (John 21:22). John's gospel then deals with a rumour that this statement had implied that John would live long enough to see the second coming of Jesus; it points out that Jesus only said, '*If* I want him to remain alive until I return, what is that to you?' The point is that Peter was challenged to make his own response, and not to keep looking over his shoulder to see what others might be doing. That is Christ's challenge still.

Ruth Bell Graham tells of an Indian student called Pashi; he was presented with the Christian message and said that he would have liked to believe in Christ, but, he said, he had never seen a Christian who was like Christ. Mrs Graham mentioned this to an Indian Christian who had at one time been President of a School of Islamic Studies in New Delhi. 'What would you say to him?' she asked. Akbar said, 'I would tell him, "I am not offering you Christians. I am offering you Christ."'[10]

This is a fair comment. The issue is the issue of truth. The basic and all-important question is not the question of how adequately or inadequately the Christian church has represented Christ; the real question is the question of whether Jesus Christ was (and is) who he said he was. The challenge to faith and discipleship comes from Jesus himself. If people were required to wait until they saw a perfect Christian before they ever trusted in Christ, there wouldn't ever have been any Christians in the world.

But the same principle could be applied to many areas of life. If you judged car-driving on the basis of the mistakes people make or the road offences people commit, you would never venture out on the roads at all. But you accept the fact that people are human and sometimes make mistakes, and you still drive your car. Again, think of medicine. Medical science has advanced so wonderfully and has become such a boon to the human race. It has also at times been grossly abused. Nazi doctors, for example, abused their medical training in vile experiments. Yet nobody refuses to avail himself or herself of the benefits of modern medicine because of this undeniable fact that some awful things have been done in the name of medicine.

And when it comes to Christianity, it is the question of truth that matters. True, there have been wicked things done in the name of Christianity at different times – but that does not settle the question of whether the thing is true or not.

Consider this vigorous expression of the point by Alister McGrath:

> It may be that a friend of mine, who is utterly charming and caring, believes passionately that the world is flat, whereas another, whom even the most generous of critics would regard as at best combining the personal charm of Attila the Hun with the intellectual ability of a stuffed frog, believes with equal passion that the world is spherical.

Sadly, the latter is correct, even if he is something of a pain. Negative personal or historical associations do not necessarily mean that a belief is wrong.[11]

In summary

In response to the assertion that disenchantment with Christians or the church is a barrier to belief, we have pointed out firstly, that the church is made up of ordinary, sinful human beings; secondly, that the issue is whether the gospel of Christ is making a difference for the better in their lives. Then thirdly, we have pointed to instances of Christianity having a very positive influence on the world; fourthly, we have emphasised that Christianity offers not Christians but Christ – the challenge is to respond to *him*.

Notes

1. Quoted by J. Drane, *Evangelism For A New Age* (Marshall Pickering, London, 1994), p.209.
2. *Understanding The Times* (Saint Andrew Press, Edinburgh, 1995), p.26.
3. S. Gaukroger, *It Makes Sense* (Scripture Union, London, 1987), p.75.
4. In 'Address to the Unco Guid', *Complete Poetical Works of Burns* (Scottish Daily Express, Glasgow, 1938).
5. S. Gaukroger, op. cit., p.81.
6. R. Skynner and J. Cleese, *Families And How To Survive Them* (Methuen, London, 1983), pp.131ff.
7. M. Green, *Man Alive!* (InterVarsity Press, London, 1967), pp.48f.
8. From *David Livingstone 1813-1873*, a booklet produced by the Church of Scotland Overseas Council for the Livingstone Centenary Scottish Inter-Church Group in 1973.
9. A. Martin in Scripture Union's *Encounter With God*, 12 January 1995.
10. R. Graham, *Legacy of a Magpie* (Hodder & Stoughton, London, 1989), p.141.
11. A. McGrath, *Bridge-Building* (IVP, Leicester, 1992), p.102.

Chapter 9

The Dullest Experience We Have?

The title for this chapter comes from a statement attributed to the entertainer, Noel Edmonds: 'The church is the dullest experience that we have in this country.'[1] No doubt he speaks for many people.

Understanding The Times says that if any one word was found more frequently than any other in the responses about barriers to belief it was the word 'boring'. This is another aspect of that disenchantment with the church which is revealed as a major barrier to Christian belief today. 'People referred to services as rigid, formal, too ceremonial, with irrelevant music and relying too much on the tradition of a time and society long past.'[2]

After quoting Noel Edmonds' statement, Stephen Gaukroger goes on to comment:

> This is one of the main reasons why people are put off Christianity. Television often shows clergymen as fanatical bigots or wet, effeminate wimps who wouldn't harm a fly. Church congregations seem to consist mainly of elderly women. They meet in old buildings and participate in some obscure ritual called worship, which involves little more than entering the building, singing a few hymns and

being asked to part with some of your hard-earned money to help prevent the steeple falling down. A club with three rules – turn up, sing up and cough up!

What are we to say to this claim that the boringness of the church is a barrier to belief? In this chapter, we will suggest three lines of response.

1. It shouldn't be boring

A ministerial colleague once posed the question, 'Whoever fell asleep at the reading of a will?'[3] He was making the point that the gathering of Christians should be an excited and exciting thing – and yet we have to admit that the sad truth is that the church has often succeeded in making it all seem dull and boring. This is a matter for deep contrition on the part of the church and of its leaders in particular.

The life of the church and its corporate activity and worship certainly ought not to be boring, for, after all, the Christian claim is that the church's message is the best news imaginable. It is not just some take-it-or-leave-it theory that doesn't make any difference to anything (OK for those who go in for that kind of thing), but rather a message which we claim is just the kind of wonderful good news that human beings need.

Consider the biblical testimony on the subject. Jesus said that the Kingdom of heaven is like 'treasure hidden in a field. When a man found it, he hid it again, and then in his joy went and sold all he had and bought that field' (Matt. 13:44).

He followed that with: 'The Kingdom of heaven is like a merchant looking for pearls of great price. When he found one of great value, he went away and sold everything he had and bought it' (Matt. 13:45).

The whole Bible is about such a discovery. It was 'treasure' for Matthew, Peter, Thomas and the rest of them – people very different from one another, but people who responded to Jesus' challenge to follow him and enter into a life of adventure and challenge – by no means an easy life, but certainly not a boring life.

Consider this passage from Paul's letter to the Ephesians, as expressed in the colourful paraphrase of Eugene Peterson. It conveys something of the excitement of one who was thrilled by the wonder of the gospel message:

> How blessed is God! And what a blessing he is! He's the Father of our Master, Jesus Christ, and takes us up to the high places of blessing in him. Long before he laid down earth's foundations, he had us in mind, had settled on us as the focus of his love, to be made whole and holy by his love. Long, long ago he decided to adopt us into his family through Jesus Christ. (What pleasure he took in planning this!) He wanted us to enter into the celebration of his lavish gift-giving by the hand of his beloved Son. Because of the sacrifice of the Messiah, his blood poured out on the altar of the Cross, we're a free people – free of penalties and punishments chalked up by all our misdeeds. And not just barely free, either. *Abundantly* free! He thought of everything, provided for everything we could possibly need, letting us in on the plans he took such delight in making.... It's in Christ that we find out who we are and what we are living for. Long before we first heard of Christ and got our hopes up, he had his eye on us, had designs on us for glorious living, part of the overall purpose he is working out in everything and for everyone (Eph. 1:3ff.).

Whatever else be said about these words, they clearly come from someone who was excited about what had come home to him. If anyone had suggested to Paul that the celebration of such things might be dull, I am sure he would have reacted with amazed incredulity; we might imagine him saying, 'Boring? You've got to be kidding!'

Later in that first chapter of Ephesians, he sets down his prayer for his readers – that they might 'grasp the immensity of this glorious way of life he has for Christians, oh, the utter extravagance of his work in us who trust him – endless energy, boundless strength!' (Eph. 1:18f.; Peterson).

Christianity is exciting good news. This is a message which, in its teaching about grace and forgiveness, deals with that fundamental flaw which lies at the heart of human experience and which messes up life in this world.

It is a message which, in its teaching about purpose and meaning, deals with that awful sense of meaninglessness which afflicts so many of our contemporaries, like the young lecturer who spoke of the pain and desolation he had experienced with the breakdown of his marriage. He said, 'At least for once in my life I knew what it meant to be loved. I would give everything for it to happen again.'[4]

We are made in such a way that we cry out for real relationships with other people, and yet we inhabit a world with much fragmentation and little communication, a world in which people interact more and more with square screens and less and less with other human beings.

We are also made in such way that our hearts cry out for a relationship with the living God, and the Christian message, in its teaching about God's love for us, and also about the reality of Christian love and fellowship, answers to these deep needs.

Let me cite one other witness: Professor James S. Stewart, speaking about Revelation 2:8-11 and especially the words, 'I know your poverty, but you are rich', said:

> This might be called the very signature tune of the New Testament. The New Testament is not a dull treatise on ethical theism or mild humanitarianism or respectable behaviour. It is much more like a wild treasure island story, throbbing with the exhilaration of stupendous discovery, fabulous wealth, colossal unsearchable riches.[5]

If all of this is so, then it is a strange and terrible thing that we should make it seem boring.

James Stewart went on: 'The trouble is that we will not believe it. Hence you get the appalling difference between the magnificent audacity of the Church's creed and the dull conventionality of its life.' May God forgive us for ever giving cause for people to say that the church is boring; may God give us grace to show forth this gospel of Jesus Christ for the breath of fresh air it truly is.

This is our first point about the charge that 'Church is boring': it certainly shouldn't be like that.

2. It isn't always like that

We have already referred to the beliefs and the excitement of the early church. When the New Testament describes the actual worshipping life of that early church, it says: 'They devoted themselves to the apostles' teaching and to the fellowship, to the breaking of bread and to prayer.' These were the features of their fellowship. It talks about miracles happening; it talks about them sharing their possessions according to need; it talks about them meeting together every day in the temple courts. 'They broke bread in their homes and ate together with glad and sincere hearts, praising God and enjoying the favour of all the people. And the Lord added to their number daily those who were being saved' (Acts 2:42-47).

Nobody could have accused that church of being boring. There was an excitement, an exhilaration, a sense of adventure which put paid to any ideas of Christianity as something akin to paying your taxes (something you know you have to do but you don't particularly like it), or to going to the dentist (something you maybe need to do for your health's sake but you don't exactly thrill with excitement at the prospect). It was more like going to a party. That is indeed the illustration Jesus used (Luke 14:16ff.), and what we know of the life of the early church bears out the aptness of it.

If people say, 'Church is boring' – well, it certainly wasn't so in the beginning.

But we have made the assertion that it *isn't* (not just wasn't) always like that. We have made the point already that the church, and especially its ministers and worship leaders, need seriously to face the challenge presented by this series of barriers to belief, and do everything possible to remove them. That may mean change.

There may be some church members who wish that the church had stuck to the Authorised Version of the Bible and only used traditional hymns which everyone knows. But even if our message has not changed, the world into which we proclaim it has changed, and changes may be called for in the way we present the message.

In fact, most churches *have* changed considerably – perhaps more than their critics realise. It might even be suggested that some of those who make these allegations about the church being boring have possibly not been in a church for a long time; we would suggest that some at least of such criticism is based on ignorance, or on memories of a long-gone atmosphere of solemnity and gloominess (maybe if people tell you the church is boring, it might be worth asking when they were last in a church).

Paul Weston suggests that we need to admit that sometimes the church looks more dead than alive, but he says:

> Thank God this isn't the whole story. For every dead church you take me to, I could take you to many that are alive with the reality of the living God. Places where God's truth is taught from the Bible. Places where there is a realism about our world. Places where the Spirit of God is active, helping people to understand what the truth about God means in their everyday lives, and enabling them to love each other as they themselves receive God's love. Places where people are finding the living God.[6]

It is also true that there are many parts of the world today where the cause of Christ is progressing by leaps and bounds, places like Kenya where the church had five thousand people at the beginning of this century and now has eight million, or like Korea where there are churches in which there are more people every Sunday than you would find at Hampden on cup final day.

Paul Weston writes, 'Some churches *are* dead! But you should no more judge Christianity on this basis than you should imagine that because one cinema has been turned into a bingo hall, the film industry is dead!' [7]

I remember a particular premier division football match I attended last year – talk about boring! I say so, not just because 'my' team was defeated, but it was the kind of game where a ball-boy playing 'keepie-uppie' with a ball on his head proved more interesting than the actual game! The atmosphere both on the park and in the stands was terrible, and really, if that was an advert for football, it didn't say much for it.

But if I drew the conclusion, 'Football is boring', someone would say to me, 'Don't judge the sport by one poor match.' Of course people can refer to bad experiences they have had of the church, but they shouldn't judge Christianity on that basis.

Perhaps the church should be readier than it often is to emphasise the positive, to point out, for example, that there are more people in church every Sunday than there are at all the country's football matches on a Saturday (it is estimated as seven times more).

A similar point was made by the Anglican Bishop of Oxford when he remarked on the fact that the Tory Party, with all its resources, could scarcely raise £3,000,000 from its members in a year when the Diocese of Oxford alone received £7,000,000 from the givings of its members.[8] Such an emphasis on the positive is something we need, and need more vigorously to publicise.

We have suggested, in response to the charge that 'Church is boring', that it shouldn't be like that and that it isn't always like that.

3. It needn't be like that

A great deal depends on the attitude with which people approach the church and its public services. If people go and they expect, or are even determined, to be bored, then bored they will be. They may spend the time counting panes of stained glass or doing equations with the numbers on the hymn-board.

We would urge people to approach the church with the real desire to find out more about this message of Jesus Christ. If you go with such a positive attitude, you may be surprised what you get out of it. You may find that things are not so stuffy as you might have expected. And maybe you will ask questions about the commitment of those you find there: what is it that makes these people disturb their Sunday long-lie and get themselves out to church week after week? Why are they so keen on it?

It is certainly the church's task to provoke such questions. The late David Watson wrote,

> All too often people are not asking questions about God at all. They are simply apathetic. But when you begin to see ordinary men and women absorbed in something, excited about something, joyful about something, singing about something, you will naturally want to know what that something is.[9]

Indeed, it needn't be boring – quite the reverse – if you discover that Christ gives purpose instead of aimlessness, pardon instead of guilt, peace instead of turmoil.

There is a stage at which children see nothing in romance and feel no attraction to the opposite sex. It may indeed be regarded as a perfectly acceptable and healthy thing if they say in exasperation, 'Boys!' or 'Girls!' – maybe children are rushed into adolescence and adulthood too quickly and not given time to be children. But usually a change takes place. Their outlook is transformed and what was boring and incomprehensible is now thrilling and very interesting.

Many have experienced such a change of attitude about worship.

A postscript

As a postscript to the consideration of the 'barrier' of the church, we should perhaps also reflect on the way in which the church in our era suffers from the disdain which is felt for many of the institutions of society which were once respected and even regarded as above criticism.

It is certainly true that the church is meant to be more than 'an institution'. It is meant to be a family, a fellowship, a living organism. But we cannot escape our history, and that history has involved the close association of the church and the state. Ours is a generation which does not give automatic respect to anyone or anything. The state, patriotism, politics, the monarchy, the law, and even parental authority are all commonly held in low esteem, and it is perhaps not surprising that the church also should suffer from this disrespect. An interviewee in *Life And Work* was asked what he believed to be the greatest challenge facing the church today. He replied, 'To survive the dark night engulfing all the great institutions of our society and still emerge with a new generation of followers.'[10]

This is a challenge to a body like the church, and, for those who are committed to it, a reminder of the importance of trusting and following Jesus Christ personally. It is not just a matter of being a member of 'a great institution', but of the fellowship of Jesus Christ whose expressed will was that his followers should, in the power of his Holy Spirit, be his witnesses in ever-widening circles, seeking to make disciples in all nations (Acts 1:8; Matt. 28:19).

Notes

1. Quoted by S. Gaukroger, *It Makes Sense* (Scripture Union, London, 1987), p.121.
2. *Understanding The Times* (Saint Andrew Press, Edinburgh, 1995), p.28.
3. A. Shaw, then minister of Gardenstown Parish Church.
4. In UCCF magazine, *NB*, April/May 1995.
5. J. S. Stewart, *The Wind of the Spirit* (Hodder & Stoughton, London, 1968), p.183.
6. P. Weston, *Why We Can't Believe* (IVP, Leicester, 1991), p.57.
7. Ibid., p.56.
8. N. McCulloch, *Barriers to Belief* (Darton, Longman & Todd, London, 1968), p.43.
9. D. Watson, *I Believe in Evangelism* (Hodder & Stoughton, London, 1976), p.31.
10. S. Lamont in *Life And Work*, November 1996, p.42.

Chapter 10

Contented Worldliness

So far the barriers to belief which we have considered have been those connected with 'intellectual' issues (suffering, science and exclusivism), with the secular climate around us and with the church (its allegedly hypocritical representatives, shady history and boring services).

The other category of barrier which came up in the 1993 survey was not so much a barrier *to* belief as simply the lack of any feeling of need for what Christianity offers. The section of *Understanding The Times* which sets out this issue has the sub-sections:

- ignorance
- apathy
- self-sufficiency

In some cases there is no knowledge of Christianity, in some cases no interest in Christianity and in other cases no sense of need for Christianity.

It is interesting to find that, as long ago as 1942, John Baillie wrote, 'The failure of the sense of need is to a large extent responsible for the failure of the belief.'[1] If that was true then, it is no doubt more so now.

In one of C. S. Lewis's famous *Screwtape Letters*, that cleverly-devised series of communications from the devil to his agents about how to evangelise for 'Our Father Below', Screwtape writes:

> You say you are 'delirious with joy' because the European humans have started another of their wars... of course war is entertaining. The immediate fear and suffering of the humans is a legitimate and pleasing refreshment for our myriads of toiling workers.... But, if we are not careful, we shall see thousands turning in their tribulation to the Enemy.... How disastrous for us is the continual remembrance of death that war enforces. One of our best weapons, contented worldliness, is rendered useless.[2]

'Contented worldliness' is probably an accurate characterisation of the attitude of many of our contemporaries today.

A minister who was on study leave had an interesting experience one Sunday as a result of a broken alternator in his car. Because of the breakdown, he stumbled into a 'place of worship' which was

> very busy, lively, warm and welcoming. Parking was relatively easy and as time passed more and more people gathered together. There were people of all ages, people on their own, families sharing together – mums, daughters, sons, even dads! The great majority seemed to be enjoying the whole experience, getting involved... at ease with what they were about.[3]

What was this attractive place of worship? It was the Gyle shopping centre on the outskirts of Edinburgh! Such shopping malls have been described as icons of our time, modern cathedrals of materialism, symbols of today's contented worldliness – obviously not doing anybody any harm, but not having any time for 'religion'.

West Lothian Presbytery said that the main barrier to belief today is 'generally a self-sufficient attitude in society, where people feel they can get by very well on their own without any need for religious faith', and it is the kind of thing we hear sometimes from eminent people.

In a radio interview the broadcaster, Ludovic Kennedy, for example, gave as his experience:

> I was brought up a Christian but now I don't feel the need for it. I didn't feel that it had any meaningful purpose in my life and I finally rejected it. The relief was enormous. I have come to the belief that all religions are man-made. It is not God who created men but men who have created gods all through their history. And therefore I can get by without religion.

Such an expression of the lack of need for Christianity would be typical of many of our contemporaries. Some of them would argue against faith, and try to lead others away from it, while others would take the line that it's all right for people who like that sort of thing – 'but it's just not for me; I have no need of it.'

What can we say?

I want to suggest three things we need to consider in relation to this 'barrier'. The first is the simple logical consideration that the absence of a sense of need makes no difference to the reality of a need, and it is folly to ignore a need because it is 'unfelt'. The second is the consideration that, even if people feel no need of 'religion' at the present time, there may come a time when they do feel such a need. These two factors will be considered in this chapter, and then in the final chapter we will turn to a third consideration, namely that such talk of a lack of need is odd when we are talking about something as thrilling as the message of Christianity.

Real needs

The first point is that needs exist, whether they are 'felt needs' or not. It is not difficult to establish this general principle. There are many things in life which we need, whether or not we *feel* any need of them.

Those who are parents know this very well. Who ever heard of a young child saying, 'Mummy, Daddy, I think it's time you took me along to the health centre to get a doctor to stick a sharp needle in my arm so that I don't get diphtheria or polio when I'm older'? Children don't *feel* any need at all, nor do they generally like the experience (as the cries will testify to those waiting outside). Yet parents put their little ones through it. Why? Not to be cruel and hurt them, but to protect them and to do the best for them.

Again, do we as a society listen to children who say, 'I don't feel any need to go to school'? Do we not rather regard education as such a good and desirable thing that we insist on children being educated, whether they like it or not?

Think of dentistry; should you wait until you have a felt need? Obviously it's better to have your teeth looked after regularly, before you're lying awake half the night with toothache.

Or, to take one other illustration of the general principle, when my car was due for its last MOT test, I didn't *feel* any need for it. The car seemed to be working well, but there were in fact several faults which needed to be rectified. If I had acted on my lack of any 'felt need' of having the car serviced, then, apart from the fact that the law would eventually catch up with me, the likelihood is that sooner or later the car would break down. In all of these areas, there *is* a need, whether people feel it or not:

- the baby needs his or her inoculations

- children need to go to school

- our teeth need looking after

- cars need attention to be kept road-worthy

The Bible's teaching, of course, is that, when it comes to our spiritual health and wellbeing, we human beings have a need, even when we don't feel it (indeed even that that very lack of a sense of need is part of the problem for which we need help).

A crutch?

A boy who has cerebral palsy referred to people who say that Christianity is a crutch for people to lean on. He boldly went on to accept that; a crutch is something to give you support, and that is exactly what Christianity does.[4] Only, we do not believe it is true because it gives such support; we believe it gives such support because it is true – because its claims about the Creator God, about the fallen-ness of human beings, about the saving activity of Jesus Christ,

about the reality of his presence, power and peace are all
true.

The point has sometimes been made that Christians
place so much emphasis on what Christianity can do for
people that they forget to argue for its truth. It is claimed
that the gospel is good news which brings comfort,
psychological well-being, happiness and so on. It may be
that the claims of Christianity present themselves to many
people along paths other than those of logic and
truthfulness, but, whatever be the initial spark, it must
sooner or later come to the issue of truth. It is not a case of
looking to Christianity as a crutch in some imaginary way
that sits light to whether it is true or not.

Make-believe?

In *Brideshead Revisited*, one character is talking to
another about his beliefs:

'But, my dear Sebastian, you can't seriously *believe* it
all?'

'Can't I?'

'I mean about Christmas and the star and the three
kings and the ox and the ass.'

'Oh, yes, I believe that. It's a lovely idea.'

'But you can't *believe* things because they're a lovely
idea.'

'But *I do*. That's how I believe.'[5]

It's a passage which reminds one of Alice in
Wonderland saying, 'There's no use trying; one *can't*
believe impossible things', and hearing the White Queen's
answer: 'I daresay you haven't had much practice. When I
was your age, I always did it for half an hour a day. Why,
sometimes I have believed as many as six impossible things
before breakfast.'

In real life, it is said that Napoleon had a curious habit of deliberately exaggerating the number of his troops and even giving out orders to divisions which didn't exist. When anyone challenged him about it, he would ask, 'Would you rob me of my peace of mind?'[6]

Perhaps many people imagine that Christians are indulging in such make-believe, telling one another nice stories to cheer themselves up and give them some sense of meaning and purpose to life.

But in fact the Bible has nothing to do with such wishful thinking and self-delusion.

We might take as typical the statement made by Luke at the beginning of his gospel. He wrote:

> Many have undertaken to draw up an account of the things that have been fulfilled among us, just as they were handed down to us by those who from the first were eye-witnesses and servants of the word. Therefore, since I myself have carefully investigated everything from the beginning, it seemed good also to me to write an orderly account for you, most excellent Theophilus, so that you may know the certainty of the things you have been taught (Luke 1:1-4).

There can be no denying the concern there expressed for accuracy of recording after careful scientific investigation. Eugene Peterson's paraphrase brings out the sense of the last verse there: 'I decided to write it all out for you so you can know beyond the shadow of a doubt the reliability of what you were taught.'

What if it were true?

Ravi Zacharias tells the story of a group of anglers on a weekend fishing trip. On the Sunday, the Christian members of the group got up early to go to church, and 'as they tiptoed past their serenely slumbering mates, one of them muttered, "Wouldn't it be awful if it turned out they were right!"'[7]

I imagine that most believing people, if they are honest, would admit that they have known such moments, moments when they have thought, 'Is it all really true, or are we just wasting our time paying attention to this message of Christ?'

Part of the answer to that is to stand it on its head – to say to the unbelieving sceptic, 'But what if the Bible is right, what if Christianity really is "true truth", what if you're missing the whole point of life in this world?'

C. S. Lewis confessed, 'Now that I am a Christian, I do have moods in which the whole thing looks very improbable; but when I was an atheist I had moods in which Christianity looked terribly probable.'[8]

This is the Christian challenge to those who say they don't feel any need of it. Our claim, the Bible's claim, is that Christianity is dealing with reality – not some imaginary world of make-believe, but the real world. Its claim is to be dealing with the ultimate issues of life and death, and if that is so, then statements about whether you feel the need of it are not the point.

Such an assertion may seem to some today to be odd, old-fashioned or out-of-touch. The 'postmodern' outlook which is adopted by many (whether consciously or unconsciously) tends to reject the concept of absolute truth. Tolerance is regarded by many as *the* great virtue, and the politically correct view is that the only thing not to be tolerated is intolerance. 'Whether it's roller blinds, ravioli or religion – what matters most is that I should be able to choose the variety that suits me.'[9] For many the feel-good factor is what matters, rather than any concept of what is *true*.

The question might well be posed: how can the statement that there is no absolute truth be regarded as true? If the premise is granted, then that statement itself must be meaningless. But certainly, for the postmodernist, the rejection of absolutes in truth, meaning and morality is taken for granted.

Gene Veith underlines the pervasiveness of such attitudes:

> Postmodernist tenets may seem academic and somewhat arcane, but they are being taught throughout contemporary universities. The new generation of college graduates has been immersed in this kind of thinking. Our new teachers, journalists, lawyers, judges and political leaders have been indoctrinated. Many of them are coming out convinced that there is no objective meaning and that truth is nothing more than an act of power.[10]

Many incidents which have happened in Britain in recent years have seemed to provoke an awareness of a need for some kind of moral renewal. The murder of young James Bulger seemed to make the nation sit up and think – for a while.

Tragically, however, our newspapers continue to carry stories of dreadful violence and murder. There are periodic calls for some kind of action to put a stop to such things.

But how – and why? In chapter 6 we noted the sad reality that our society as a whole seems to have drifted so far from any kind of agreed basis for morality that it is difficult to find *any* basis for the kind of renewal that seems to be demanded. If someone who wants to use a knife as a weapon were to ask the question '*Why* should I refrain from doing this?' the harsh reality is that there is little well-argued response other than: those of us who believe that it is wrong to do so are greater in number and power than those who think there's nothing wrong with such behaviour. In the absence of any belief in objective truth, it is to be feared that this argument of power is the only rationale for 'good' behaviour.

Some time ago, there were reports of moves to decriminalise sado-masochism; it was argued that if consenting adults wish to inflict pain on each other, there should be no attempt to stop them doing so. (Interestingly, the European Court of Justice in 1997 ruled that interference with the right to privacy is justified as necessary for the protection of health.)

But one of the characteristics of the discussion of the matter has been the lack of any objective *moral* standard; such issues tend to be discussed simply in terms of personal preferences. Some people have raised the question: what if people then go on to inflict pain on children or young people in the belief (honest or otherwise) that they were consenting – or for that matter, even against their will? Obviously (and thankfully) most people would regard such things with utter abhorrence, but the hard question might be posed: what if a time should come when the majority of people believe that there would be nothing wrong in such practices? What if the steady efforts of some campaigners are as successful in changing society's view as they have been in (say) the area of homosexuality within the last ten or twenty years? (Has there ever been such an over-turning of the outlook of a society within such a brief period?) It is unpleasant even to think of such things, but the bottom-line question must be: is it to be simply a matter of majority votes and the exercise of power?

'A time may come...'

To return to our main theme, the fact that people do not *feel* a need for Christianity does not affect the question of the reality of such a need.

The other thing we would mention in this chapter is that, even if people do not feel a need of Christianity now, there may well come a time when they will come to such a realisation.

We referred earlier to one of Jesus' famous stories, in which he described two people building their lives on very different foundations. At the end of the Sermon on the Mount, he said (Matt. 7:24): 'Everyone who hears these words of mine and puts them into practice is like a wise man who built his house on the rock. The rain came down, the streams rose, and the winds blew and beat upon that house; yet it did not fall, because it had its foundation on the rock.'

He contrasted that with the case of the 'foolish man' who had his house built in no time at all; it was wonderful how quickly it went up. But then when the storm came, that house 'fell with a great crash'.

Clearly, the adverse circumstances – the rain falling, the stream rising, the wind blowing – represent the stresses and strains of life which will sooner or later come to us, and which will reveal the truth about our lives. And, Jesus was saying, what a tragic thing it is if people find then that their house crumbles under the strain.

Everything was fine for the man who built his house on sand so long as the weather was fine. But when the storm broke, the difference was revealed.

The message is clear: 1 Corinthians 3:13 talks about how 'The day will declare it' – meaning that great day when Christ comes again and when we must all appear before his judgement-seat. But even before that Day (with a capital D) there may be many days that will declare the truth about what we have been building.

The Bible's message is: now is the important time, because what will be revealed then is what you are building now. No-one would wait until their house was on fire before trying to arrange an insurance policy, would they? It is folly to wait. That is the contrast in Jesus' parable: the wise man and the foolish man.

The contrast is not between someone who hears the message of Christ and someone who does not. The contrast is between 'everyone who hears these words of mine and puts them into practice' and 'everyone who hears these words of mine and does not put them into practice'.

Today we have the situation in which many people haven't really heard the message of Christ – and we're not just talking about people living in remote regions to which no missionary has yet gone. *Understanding The Times* reports:

> Lack of knowledge, especially among younger people, is a factor mentioned by several Presbyteries. Increasing numbers of people are very ignorant about even the basic story of Jesus's life, teaching, death and resurrection.[11]

James Philip suggests:

> we have come to a situation of general and widespread ignorance of the Scriptures and of the essence of the Faith as great as anything since pre-Reformation times.[12]

Understanding The Times goes on to suggest that the church's reaction should not be to criticise people for being ignorant, or say things like 'fancy them not knowing *that*' – but rather to take it seriously and find ways of telling the story again.

Through the parable, Jesus was saying: 'Everyone who hears these words of mine and puts them into practice is like a wise man who built his house on rock.' And his point is: don't wait until trouble comes; now is the time to build a house which will withstand whatever rains may fall, whatever floods may rise, whatever winds may blow and beat upon your house.

Loss of appetite

Our last chapter will give one other answer to this 'barrier' of the lack of a sense of need for Christianity. For now, let us close this chapter with one other analogy – loss of appetite. That is a feature of some illnesses. Can we imagine medical staff saying to a patient who doesn't want to eat, 'That's OK, if you don't feel like eating anything, just don't bother'? No, they would be concerned – they might encourage, coax, spoon-feed or, if need be, drip-feed – because the lack of taste for food makes no difference whatsoever to the *need* for food.

It is a good analogy, because this is what the Bible would say about spiritual hunger too. Many people today are 'off their food', but that doesn't mean they don't need it. Maybe they don't have a feeling of hunger, but without food they will die.

Notes

1. J. Baillie, *Invitation to Pilgrimage* (Oxford University Press, London, 1942), p.80.
2. C. S. Lewis, *The Screwtape Letters* (Collins, London & Glasgow, 1942), pp. 29, 32.
3. J. Simpson, 'Guile and the Gospel', *Ministers' Forum* 174 (May 1995), p.1.
4. In the video, *The Edge,* from The National Bible Society of Scotland, 1993.
5. Evelyn Waugh, *Brideshead Revisited* (David Campbell Publishers, London, 1993), p.76.
6. A. J. Gossip, *The Hero in thy Soul* (T&T Clark, Edinburgh, 1928), p.245.
7. R. Zacharias, *A Shattered Visage* (Baker, Grand Rapids, Michigan, 1990), p.1.
8. C. S. Lewis, *Mere Christianity* (Collins, London & Glasgow, 1952), p.121.
9. G. Cray, *The Gospel and Tomorrow's Culture* (CPAS, Warwick, 1994), p.6
10. G. Veith, *Guide to Contemporary Culture* (Crossway, Leicester, 1994), pp.50f.
11. *Understanding The Times* (Saint Andrew Press, Edinburgh, 1995), p.11.
12. *Record* of Holyrood Abbey, November 1995, p.5.

Chapter 11

Good News

In the last chapter we considered the kind of 'barrier' which is presented by the lack of a sense of need for Christianity – the kind of attitude expressed by the well-known Professor Richard Dawkins of Oxford, who is one of Britain's most prominent spokesmen for atheism. In a broadcast interview, Sheena McDonald asked him about the vacuum that would exist if there were no religion. He answered:

> I feel no vacuum; I feel very happy, very fulfilled. I love my life, and I love all sorts of aspects of it which have nothing to do with my science. So I don't have a vacuum. I don't feel cold and bleak; I don't think the world is a cold and bleak place. I think the world is a lovely and a friendly place, and I enjoy being in it. We must live life to the full in this life, because there's nothing else.[1]

So far, in seeking to respond to such a barrier, we have suggested that needs may be real even if they are unrecognised and that even if people do not feel a need for Christianity now, there may come a time when they do feel such a need.

In this chapter we would suggest that the assertion of a lack of need really misses the point. Christianity's claim is that Christ enriches life; its claim is that faith adds a new dimension to our existence; it claims to be good news.

Good news

Suppose you have just found out that you have been left a fortune by that legendary great-uncle in some far-off country. You had never heard of him, but a letter comes from a solicitor's office to tell you that he has left his fortune to you. It is highly unlikely that you would say, 'Oh, but I don't feel any need of that', or 'I have no interest in it.' There would probably be a great sense of excitement about it. It might be true that, up till then, you had not felt any *need* of such a fortune – but that is irrelevant now.

This kind of experience came, according to the '100 years ago' column of the Banffshire Journal, to an old inmate of the Lambeth Workhouse. The report said, 'By a singular freak of fortune, a Lambeth pauper named Sheridan has become the heir to real and personal property valued at £300,000.'[2] It would have been very strange indeed if Mr Sheridan had said, 'I'm not interested in that', or, 'I don't feel any need of it.'

Christianity claims to be such good news that it becomes irrelevant to talk about the lack of a sense of need for it. It is good news: news of One who came into our world to deal with that flaw in our human make-up which leads to so much trouble and discord in human life. It is sometimes stated that the heart of the human problem is the problem of the human heart, and Jesus Christ said that he had come to deal with that problem of the heart. It is, he said, from the heart that there come 'evil thoughts, murder, adultery, sexual immorality, theft, false testimony, slander' (Matt. 15:19), and the Bible is all about the promise of a new heart. Paul expressed the gospel message in these terms: 'If anyone is in Christ, he is a new creation; the old has gone, the new has come!' (2 Cor. 5:17).

In two of the chapters of John's gospel we find this message of new life expressed in terms of two very different people. In John 3, we meet Nicodemus, a religious and upright man, who came to Jesus by night, presumably because he didn't want to be seen coming to Jesus. He had certain questions to put to Jesus, and it is at the heart of that conversation that we find Jesus' famous message about being born again.

In John 4, we then meet the un-named Samaritan woman, who turned out to be so different from Nicodemus. She was a woman with a turbulent background, having been married five times and then cohabiting with another man. And it was to her that Jesus said (referring first to the water of Jacob's well), 'Everyone who drinks this water will be thirsty again, but whoever drinks the water I give him will never thirst. Indeed, the water I give him will become in him a spring of water welling up to eternal life' (John 4:13-14).

Christ's message is not simply good advice but good news of the change he can make, and his disciples went out to spread the news.

Good news about Jesus

Their message centred on the incarnation, death and resurrection of Jesus himself. By his incarnation Christ identified himself with us. He came to deal with our problems from the inside and Christianity seeks to take full account of both the humanity and the deity of Jesus. He was fully human. The gospels tell of him experiencing hunger and thirst, sadness and joy (as the children's Christmas carol says, 'Tears and smiles like us he knew'). He was also fully divine, and the Gospels obviously testify to that, with the frequently reiterated question, 'Who is this?' and the answer that he was none other than God incarnate (e.g. John 1:1-3; John 4:26; John 8:58; John 14:9).

Much is recorded of his life and teaching, but a large proportion of the gospel story centres on the events leading up to and culminating in his death on the cross. This death is presented not simply as a noble martyrdom, or as a model of innocent suffering patiently borne, but rather as an atoning sacrifice. We are told about God's righteous opposition to sin, and about Jesus willingly taking our sin in himself to remove it.

Ernest Gordon's story of the Argyll soldier has always seemed to me to be a fine expression of this aspect of New Testament teaching. The squad of prisoners-of-war on the infamous railway had finished their day's work, when the Japanese guard shouted that a shovel was missing. He insisted that someone had stolen it to sell it to the Thais. He worked himself up into a rage and demanded that the guilty party should step forward to receive his punishment. When no-one moved, he shrieked, 'All die! All die!' and put his rifle to his shoulder to show that he meant it. As he aimed at the first man in the line, the Argyll stepped forward and said, 'I did it.' The guard proceeded to unleash all his hatred, kicking and beating the helpless prisoner. Finally, he took his rifle by the barrel and brought it down on the skull of the Argyll. Although the soldier was obviously dead, the guard kept beating him until he was exhausted. Finally, the story says, they shouldered their tools and marched back to camp. When the tools were counted again at the guard-house, no shovel was missing.[3]

That is a story of tremendous human heroism. It is also a good picture of what the Bible says about the death of Jesus, the innocent one who took our place and won our liberty and salvation through his self-sacrifice.

But, of course, the Bible proclaims that he did not stay dead. Rumours started to circulate that he had been seen alive again, and no explanation could be discovered for the fact that the body was missing. If enemies had stolen it, they would have produced it to squash Christian claims about the resurrection; if his followers had stolen it, they would hardly have suffered martyrdom for a lie. Theories about people going to the wrong tomb, having hallucinations, the victim not actually dying on the cross – none of them stands up to examination.[4]

In modern times, the idea of a 'spiritual' resurrection has become popular (the idea that the 'spirit of Jesus' lives on in his followers). John Stott refers to this notion:

> When Paul wrote that Jesus died, was buried and was raised, he assuredly did not mean that he was raised while still remaining buried. That would make nonsense of the apostle's declaration. As Dr Earle Ellis has written, it is extremely unlikely that the earliest Palestinian Christians could have conceived of some kind of 'spiritual' resurrection: 'To them an anastasis (resurrection) without an empty grave would have been about as meaningful as a square circle.' Paul was affirming then that what was raised was what had been buried, namely the Lord's body, and that therefore the tomb was empty.[5]

Believe It Or Not!

'Blessings abound where'er he reigns'

These truths of the incarnation, crucifixion and resurrection of Jesus are at the heart of the New Testament's teaching, and it is through these once-for-all events that he offers forgiveness of our sins and failures, an assurance of his acceptance, a new sense of purpose and direction in life, and the prospect of eternal life. 'What shall I find if I accept your gospel and become Christ's man?' asked King Brude of St Brendan, and Brendan replied, 'If you become his man, you will stumble upon wonder upon wonder, and every wonder true.'[6]

It is along these lines that Christianity answers this assertion of the lack of a sense of need for the gospel. To talk in such terms is to deny yourself so much, to cut yourself off from so much that God wants to give, not demand. No doubt it is one of the great misconceptions that Christianity is all about what God demands of us (do this, do that, etc.), whereas the truth is that it is primarily about what he wants to give.

John Baillie wrote about 'the greatest misunderstanding to which religion has been subject in every age'. To what was he referring? He was referring to the notion that God is a stern taskmaster rather than a loving Father. Thinking of the words of Revelation 3:20 about Christ standing knocking at the door of people's hearts, he wrote:

> He who stands at the door has come with a gift, but we are so ready to think He has come for a payment. The knock is a Saviour's knock, but we are so ready to think it a Taskmaster's.... It is the common error of most pre-Christian and non-Christian forms of religion, and it is also the error which has done most to falsify and limit the

true understanding of Christianity itself. We turn our religion into a code of good conduct, an ideal to be striven for, a law to be obeyed.[7]

He relates an interesting story told by Charles Spurgeon about a fellow-minister who went to the house of a poor widow with a contribution of money for payment of the rent. He knocked again and again, but there was no answer. But the widow was in the house, and her explanation afterwards was, 'I heard the knocking, but I thought it was the man come to ask for the rent.'

So many people have the idea that Christianity is all about a God who demands things of us instead of realising that it is primarily about what he gives.

The demands of discipleship

It is not that we should downplay the demands of discipleship, because it is certainly true that Christ's call is a radical call for committed discipleship. He does not want admirers but followers, and sometimes that has a cost. It is not always easy to live a consistent Christian life, and Jesus himself did not soft-pedal that aspect of his teaching. To one who demurred at it, he famously did not call him back and seek to negotiate a better agreement (Matt. 19:22).

Paul summarised the radical call of Christ in Romans 12:1-2 (quoting it from Eugene Peterson's paraphrase):

Take your everyday, ordinary life – your sleeping, eating, going-to-work, and walking-around life – and place it before God as an offering. Embracing what God does for you is the best thing you can do for him. Don't become so well-adjusted to your culture that you fit into it without even thinking. Instead, fix your attention on God. You'll be changed from the inside out. Readily recognise what he wants from you, and quickly respond to it.

Ardrossan Presbytery reported, 'Some people understand the message, but feel that the cost of commitment is too much for them.' This may reflect the real feelings of many, but the point is that all that is demanded in terms of Christian discipleship is set forth as a response to the amazing grace of Christ. It is, in the words of a well-known hymn, 'love so amazing, so divine' that 'demands my soul, my life, my all'.

At least that objection about the cost of commitment does reveal a realisation about the demands of Christ's call. Michael Green has written:

> The idea has got around that to be a Christian is a soft option. Incredible! It just shows how good the Enemy's propaganda machine is. As a matter of fact, only people with courage, the folks who are prepared to swim against the current, are to be found among the committed followers of Jesus Christ. They may be little old ladies, or tough business executives, navvies or newspaper men, but they all need moral courage if they are going to stand up and be counted as the friends of Jesus.... So let's get out of our heads for good and all the 'Come to Jesus and everything in the garden will be lovely' sort of approach. If you have ever heard preachers talk like that, forget them. That is not the authentic article, but a sugary imitation of genuine Christianity.[8]

Yes, the demands of Jesus are considerable, and he did not try to hide that fact in the small print somewhere.

In this book we have been seeking to respond to the things which people identify as barriers to belief. We have enumerated them as they relate to intellectual issues, the secular climate, the church's failings and the lack of a sense of need for faith. These were the responses gained in a specific endeavour to find out what the real barriers are.

It is, however, interesting to consider also some things which were *not* reported in the returns from the different Presbyteries. Two things in particular are of some interest.

The first is the fact that there is little reference to problems with the Bible or Christian teaching. True, we came upon *some* such questions in considering the barriers presented by suffering, science and pluralism. In each of these cases, people raised questions about things contained in the Bible (e.g. the assertion that God is love, that he created everything and that Christ alone can save people). Nonetheless, it must be said that biblical and theological questions did not feature highly. Once upon a time, Christian apologists faced questions about the alleged contradictions in the Bible, or about the implications of archaeological or manuscript discoveries, but few people today raise such issues or theological questions about (say) the doctrine of the trinity, or about unanswered prayer, as barriers to belief.

The other omission concerns the moral demands of Christianity. Perhaps it was unlikely that people who were asked about the barriers that keep them from faith *would* say that the demands of Christian discipleship presented a barrier to them. But one may suspect that the lifestyle factor is a very real barrier to many.

Consider two specific examples. One is the area of sexual ethics, particularly as relating to young people.[9] Statistics say that many unmarried young people are sexually active, and it is clear that cohabitation has become very common. There is little publicity, however, for the statistical evidence that couples who live together before marriage are twice as likely to divorce as those who do not.

Another example of the moral challenge of Christianity concerns the national lottery, which has been such a huge concern of the media during its first year. It is well-known that Christianity, on biblical grounds, opposes gambling, and if it is true, as claimed by Camelot, that two out of every three people in Britain take part in the lottery, then this highlights another great difficulty in the way of Christian evangelism.

For some people, the answer to such problems is clear: Christianity must change, move with the times. They say that we must simply accept the prevalence of extra-marital sexual activity and alter our view that gambling is contrary to the mind of Christ and to responsible Christian stewardship.

Some time ago, a senior person in the Anglican Church expressed the view that unless the Church of England changes its mind on divorce, it will lose touch with the people.[10] This statement puts its finger on a crucial issue for the Church as a whole, as it seeks to relate to the times in which we live and remain faithful to its own scriptural basis.

Real Christianity is not a chameleon-like religion which changes with changing circumstances, and we are not at liberty (altering the metaphor) to change the Christian message according to the winds that blow in any particular era. It has often been said that whoever marries the spirit of this age will be widowed in the next. In any case, one might wonder what respect people would have for a church which is ready to alter its beliefs because these beliefs are unpopular. Is it not more likely that such an attitude would produce disdain and contempt rather than evangelistic success?

Such, at any rate, were some of the things which were *not* identified as barriers to belief.

And we return to the fact that Christ himself did not soft-pedal the demands of discipleship or hide them in the small print. He was up-front in his teaching, even saying, 'If anyone would come after me, he must deny himself and take up his cross and follow me' (Mark 8:34). He did not try to attract people by down-playing the cost of commitment, and if his church would be faithful to him, it cannot do so either. Sometimes the church is called to take an unpopular stand, and to set forth a radical call for people to face up to the serious demands of a faith that is neither the adoption of a patron-saint, nor 'the hero-worship we would pay to a good martyr, but obedience to the Son of God'.[11]

A party?

Still, after all of the above has been said about the demands of Christian discipleship, Jesus did also liken his kingdom to a party. He said (Matt. 22:2) 'The kingdom of heaven is like a king who prepared a wedding banquet for his son.' That is a far cry from the view many have of Christianity, but that is Jesus' own comparison. And when the people in the parable 'began with one consent to make excuses', the irony is unmistakable: excuses, when you're invited to something happy and wonderful? But these people were preoccupied; the demands of business or home were too insistent: they were not doing anything wicked; it was just that other things became like thorns that choked the seed of the Word (Matt. 13:22).

The challenge

This book has been about barriers to faith, and a well-known hymn says:

> Just as I am – Thy love unknown
> Has broken every barrier down –
> Now to be thine, yea, thine alone,
> O Lamb of God, I come.[12]

We have referred to the apathy and indifference that are so widespread, and those who are believers need to work hard at finding ways in which we can challenge people today. Perhaps there are many who feel that they should do something about the whole matter, just as there are perhaps many others who do believe and know that they ought to go further with it and be far more radical in their commitment, but something holds them back.

At the end of his excellent evangelistic book, *It Makes Sense*, Stephen Gaukroger poses this challenge:

> This means that it is perfectly possible to be convinced that it makes a lot of sense. You can see the logic of the arguments. You agree that there is a great deal of evidence to support real Christianity. *And you are probably not going to do anything about it!* It's the same reason that the forty-a-day man puffs himself to an early grave. He knows the facts about smoking, but doesn't want to (or feels he can't) change. And even if the facts are forcefully and clearly presented on a brilliantly creative video with

additional coloured brochures, we will only have succeeded in making our heavy smoker a superbly well-informed, perhaps slightly more miserable, heavy smoker! Only when he wants to change are we going to see any real action.[13]

Of course there is an ultimate mystery about it all – why one believes and another doesn't, why one is a committed Christian and another can't understand for the life of him what his friend sees in it all. There *is* a mystery, and certainly no-one can convert someone else. But, as noted earlier, the fact that it is God who gives the increase is no reason why we need not plant and water. And if we can help in any way to remove some of the barriers to belief which present themselves today, maybe we can help people towards a real faith in Christ.

One useful feature of modern life is the digital alarm clock with its snooze-button. This is a very useful device by which we can delay the trauma of getting up in the morning; we can silence the irksome sound of the buzzer by reaching out and pressing the snooze-button to give ourselves another seven minutes before it sounds again. Perhaps there are some who make this kind of response to the challenge of Christ. They intend to do something about it some day, but for the moment they just press that snooze-button again – and again.

Luke tells of one man who did this. Felix was a Roman governor who had to deal with Paul, who had been taken into custody. After adjourning the initial hearing, pending the arrival of another official, Felix called for Paul to be brought to him for an off-the-record conversation. Acts 24:24 tells us that he listened as Paul spoke about faith in Jesus Christ, but the next verse says, 'As Paul discoursed on righteousness, self-control and the judgement to come, Felix was afraid and said, "That's enough for now! You may leave. When I find it convenient, I will send for you."' In other words, he pressed the snooze-button, and when he was replaced two years later, he still hadn't done anything about it.

Paul had written earlier (Rom. 13:11) about 'understanding the present time', and he went on, 'The hour has come for you to wake up.'

The footstep in the hall, about which C. S. Lewis wrote, is not the footstep of someone who wants to spoil life for people or take things away from them. The Christian message is much more wonderful than that. It is all about a God of love and grace.

We have entitled this chapter 'Good news'. 'Gospel' means 'good news', and the claim of Christianity is that so many of the barriers to belief, including this idea that people don't feel any need of it, become irrelevant if people realise that the message of Christianity is good news. It is a sad thing if Christians have given or give the impression that Christianity is a burdensome thing, a heavy load to carry, a dismal life of dreary duty. In truth, it is far more wonderful than that.

C. S. Lewis's story, *The Lion, the Witch and the Wardrobe* conveys this message through Aslan's coming to break the power of the White Witch, under whose influence it was 'always winter but never Christmas'.[14]

After Aslan had been put to death and had come back to life, there is a delightful description of the joy brought to Lucy and Susan:

> A mad chase began. Round and round the hill-top he led them, now hopelessly out of their reach, now letting them almost catch his tail, now diving between them, now

tossing them in the air with his huge and beautifully velveted paws and catching them again, and now stopping unexpectedly so that all three of them rolled over together in a happy laughing heap of fur and arms and legs. It was such a romp as no one has ever had except in Narnia.[15]

In the filmed video version, during this 'romp' flowers sprang up wherever Aslan's feet touched the ground, reminding one of the words of a hymn based on Psalm 72:

> He shall come down like showers
> Upon the fruitful earth,
> And love, joy, hope, like flowers,
> Spring in His path to birth.[16]

This is followed in the Narnia tale by the scene in which Aslan goes to the White Witch's castle, and brings back to life the creatures who had been turned to stone. Aslan would simply breathe on them; for example, we read:

> For a second after Aslan had breathed upon him the stone lion looked just the same. Then a tiny streak of gold began to run along his white marble back – then it spread – then the colour seemed to lick all over him as the flame licks all over a bit of paper. ... Everywhere the statues were coming to life; there was a blaze of colours and the whole place rang with songs and laughter.[17]

This is a picture of the way in which Christ enriches the lives of those who put their trust in him ('For in him you have been enriched in every way' – 1 Cor. 1:5). The Christian claim is that, far from detracting from life, Christ adds a new dimension to everything.

If there is a footstep in the hall, it is not the footstep of one who comes to spoil things or cramp people's lives. Jesus himself said it is the thief who comes to steal, kill and destroy; he said, 'I have come that they may have life, and have it to the full' (John 10:10).

It is hoped that this look at some of the barriers which people say hold them back from Christianity has helped people like 'John' to take another look at the message of the gospel of Christ. 'John' is a decent person who once thought that belief in God, good citizenship and decent living all went together. But over the years different things happened, different influences came to bear upon him and different thoughts occurred to him, and they made him leave behind attitudes which he came to regard as naive. We have considered the kind of things that present barriers to belief, and hopefully found some answers, some encouragements to think again.

'There comes a moment when the children who have been playing burglars hush suddenly: was that a *real* footstep in the hall?'

Far from being the footstep of a thief or robber, it is the footstep of a Saviour and a Friend.

Notes

1. Channel 4 interview, 15 August 1994.
2. Reported in *Banffshire Journal*, 23 December 1992.
3. E. Gordon, *Miracle on the River Kwai* (Collins, Glasgow, 1963), pp.88f.
4. See, e.g., J. Wenham, *Easter Enigma* (Paternoster, Exeter, 1984).
5. J. Stott, *The Authentic Jesus* (Marshalls, Basingstoke, 1985), p.44.
6. From J. S. Stewart, sermon, 'What the Gospel Means To-Day', in *Man's Dilemma and God's Answer* (S.C.M. Press Ltd., London, 1944), pp.159-76.
7. J. Baillie, *Invitation to Pilgrimage* (Oxford University Press, London, 1942), p.48.

8. M. Green, *Why Bother with Jesus?* (Hodder & Stoughton, London, 1979), p.57.

9. In *Redemption*, October 1991, Josh McDowell has suggested that sexual activity by professing Christian young people has taken a devastating toll on discipleship, evangelism and missionary recruiting. Referring to a British background, Anne Carlos similarly says, 'many young people are so sexually compromised that they don't feel able to go into Christian service' *(Newsletter of Christian Initiative on Teenage Sexuality,* Issue 9). Since many young people reject the counsel of older people (authority figures), we might hope and pray for a British version of the movement among some American young people which advocates the keeping of sex (a God-given gift) for the committed relationship of marriage, and a rejection of the attitude that sex means little more than shaking hands.

10. Cited by D. Wright in *Rutherford Journal of Church & Ministry*, 2, 1 (1995), p.1.

11. D. Bonhoeffer, *The Cost of Discipleship* (SCM, London, 1959), p.66.

12. 'Just as I am, without one plea', by Charlotte Elliott, *Revised Church Hymnary* (Oxford University Press, Glasgow, 1929), no.411.

13. S. Gaukroger, *It Makes Sense* (Scripture Union, London, 1987), p.116.

14. C. S. Lewis, *The Lion, the Witch and the Wardrobe* (Puffin, Harmondsworth, 1950), p.23.

15. Ibid., p.148.

16. 'Hail to the Lord's Anointed' by James Montgomery, *Revised Church Hymnary* (Oxford University Press, Glasgow, 1929), no.154.

17. C. S. Lewis, op. cit., p.152f.

Chapter 12

To Believe Or Not to Believe...

That is the question which was posed at the outset of this book, and it is hoped that our consideration of the barriers to belief mentioned has encouraged 'John' to think again, and perhaps also given some help to Christians in facing the issues which friends claim prevent them believing.

'It's good to listen'

As mentioned in the introduction, the actual barriers which have formed the subject-matter of this book were all mentioned in a survey conducted under the auspices of the Church of Scotland in 1993. An attempt was made to find out what were the real issues that people saw as barriers to belief.

People spoke of so-called 'intellectual issues' (suffering, science and pluralism), of the secularism and materialism of our age, of the barrier of the church's poor representatives, bad history and boring services, and of the lack of any sense of need for what Christianity claims to offer.

The findings were reported to the General Assembly in 1995 (and subsequently published by Saint Andrew Press) under the title *Understanding The Times*. That title comes from 1 Chronicles 12:32 where a list of the followers of King

David includes some 'men of Issachar, who understood the times and knew what Israel should do'. The church needs to listen in order to understand how people think and feel in these times in which we live.

At several points we have quoted from the returns made by Presbyteries based on the surveys undertaken by their members. One Presbytery, in its report, made the comment: 'We need to continue the process (of building bridges for faith) if the reading of horoscopes is not going to take over from the reading of the Bible, and if belief in the God and Father of our Lord Jesus Christ is going to win the day against vague notions of God as a force or Mother Nature.' Another said, 'As a Church we may increasingly find that we need to show why faith should be Christian faith.'[1]

However, it should also be said that it is not a matter of the church listening in order to alter or adapt the Christian message accordingly, or of seeking to change the message to make it more popular than it is.

Luke's Gospel tells of Jesus being tempted at the very outset of his public ministry to adapt his message in ways that would 'appeal' to people. If he were to go in for sensational acts like turning stones into bread, coming to a compromise arrangement with the devil and falling from a height and landing unhurt – then what a following he could attract (Luke 4:3-9). But he turned his back on such temptations; the content and style of his ministry were not up for grabs.

Later, one of his followers would write about contending for the faith which was once-for-all entrusted to God's people (Jude 3), and the apostle Paul laid strong emphasis on the same principle. He wrote, 'the gospel I preached is not something that men made up. I did not receive it from any man, nor was I taught it; rather, I received it by revelation from Jesus Christ' (Gal. 1:11-12).

However, it is undeniable that there are vast numbers of people today who have no time for what we Christians say we have to offer. So many of our contemporaries consider our message to be outmoded, the church to be out-of-touch, and personal faith to be out of the question.

It would be a mistake to over-state this truth. The modern media often suggest that practically all churches are empty and that it is only a matter of time until Christianity is thrown aside. They share the view expressed by anthropologist Max Müller:

> Every day, every week, every month, every quarter, the most widely read journals seem just now to vie with each other in telling us that the time for religion is past, that faith is a hallucination or an infantile disease, that the gods have at last been found out and exploded.[2]

However, these words were written in 1878! It is no new thing when people imply that Christianity is on the way out.

But there is plenty of cause for concern for the church. Although this book has been concerned not simply with the question, 'Why don't you come to church?' but with the deeper and more fundamental question, 'What keeps you from Christian faith?', it is true that the church's problems can be illustrated in terms of both church membership and church attendance.

Membership of the Church of Scotland reached a peak in 1961 when there were 1,292,617 members. In 1997 the figure stood at 660,954. That is still a sizeable number of people, and there are things that can be said about the many people who were on membership rolls and only ever were nominal members, lacking a real personal faith and commitment. But there is clearly cause for concern.

When it comes to actual church attendance, the church's cause for concern has been underlined by the published results of the 1994 Attendance Census. It reveals that one in seven people in Scotland attends church, but obviously this means that six do not! Fergus Macdonald summarises the findings and makes comment as follows:

> Previous censuses reveal that there has been a steady decline in attendance since the late fifties. The proportion of the adult population in church on any given Sunday fell from 28% in 1959 to 17% in 1984 and then to 14% in 1994. Yet over these 35 years all the Scottish churches have made great strides in efficiency. Most now have computerised central records co-ordinated by highly professional staff. Most have vastly improved facilities for liaising with the media. Some have worked hard on PR and developed a modern corporate identity. Many local churches use word processors and produce their parish magazines and information bulletins with desk top publishing software. Church buildings are, on the whole, well heated, many use public address and loop hearing systems, and in a growing number hard pews have either been cushioned or replaced by comfortable chairs. But the overall result is exodus rather than influx![3]

Christians, of course, believe that the gospel is as powerful today as we enter the third millennium AD as it has ever been. The President of Princeton Theological Seminary was reflecting on the future of the 210 people graduating in May 1998:

As I looked at those graduates, I thought of the hope they offer to a church threatened by division and declining membership. I told them that although the church has been marginalised in (American) society and has in a sense entered a time of cultural exile, they must remember that no force or power at work in human history can override the work of the living God revealed in Jesus Christ.[4]

The last thing which the world needs from the church is for that church to capitulate to the world's standards, to be 'blown here and there by every wind of teaching' or even by what Paul uncomplimentarily called 'the cunning and craftiness of men in their deceitful scheming' (Eph. 4:14). The press recently reported on a survey of the willingness of various corporations and institutions to respond to public opinion. 'Burger giant McDonald's is a better listener to public opinion than the Church.... McDonald's were thought to be more willing to listen than High Street banks, the Royal Family or the Church.'[5] It is an interesting survey and an interesting conclusion, but it clearly begs the question of whether the church ought to be listening to public opinion in the sense of being ready to re-invent itself in a way that is thought to be more appealing to the modern (or postmodern) 'consumer'.

A front-bench Member of Parliament evidently thought that this should be the church's approach; she commented that the attitude of the Roman Catholic Church to abortion had cost it the support of her generation of women. Behind such a statement is the view that the Church would do better to alter its stance in order to win popularity.

This, however, is not a course open to the church. The church's allegiance must be to its Master, and to the Book that is its title-deeds, and possibly there are times when society needs the church simply to be the church. Perhaps we are in such a time, when the church needs to exercise patience – a patience which is married to evangelistic passion, but which is still patient.

However, the church must also struggle with the question of its methods and forms in the days in which we live. The message of the church is not up for grabs, but the church needs to be constantly seeking appropriate ways of putting across its message for today. Our world is a very different world today from the world of the nineteenth century or the first century. The message which Paul and the others proclaimed in a world of chariots and sailing ships is the message which needs to be proclaimed today in our world of bio-ethical issues and hedonistic permissiveness, of secularism and postmodernism.

'Open our eyes, Lord'

Some people have suggested that there is little value in investigating people's stated barriers to belief since (they say) the principal and basic barrier to belief is quite simply human self-centredness and sin. The Bible says, 'The god of this age has blinded the minds of unbelievers, so that they cannot see the light of the gospel' (2 Cor. 4:4).

The Bible would indeed say that our very analysis of the barriers which hold us back is, like every aspect of our lives, flawed; we are not necessarily reliable guides even on this subject. In the Gospels, it is often Jesus' questions that interpret to people their real needs, whether they realised them previously or not (e.g. Mark 2:5), and the letter to the Church in Laodicea in Revelation 3:14-22 puts its finger on this very point: 'You say, "I am rich; I have acquired wealth and do not need a thing." But you do not realise that you are wretched, pitiful, poor, blind and naked.' So much for the complacent self-analysis of the Laodicean Church! The great need of these people was to face up to God's diagnosis of their condition. Their town was known for its banks, its textile industry and its eye salve, but they needed to face up to the fact that spiritually they were poor, naked and blind.

It is that passage that then goes on to the wonderful statement of Christ: 'Here I am! I stand at the door and knock. If anyone hears my voice and opens the door, I will come in, and eat with him, and he with me' (Rev. 3:20).

Proclaiming or persuading?

Paul wrote in 2 Corinthians 5:11 about his endeavour to persuade people. It was not just a case of proclaiming his message in a 'take it or leave it' fashion. Obviously people were free to accept it or reject it, but, as well as vigorously proclaiming his message, Paul sought to persuade others of its truth and relevance.

Earlier in the same letter, he wrote the words we quoted already about the 'god of this age' blinding the minds of unbelievers, 'so that they cannot see the light of the gospel of the glory of Christ who is the image of God' (2 Cor. 4:4-5). He believed that there is an evil spirit who seeks to blind people's eyes to God's message. Paul did not rely on his own powers of persuasion alone. He trusted in the promised guidance and power of the Holy Spirit to help him convince others by all means.

He also said, 'We do not preach ourselves, but Jesus Christ as Lord, and ourselves as your servants for Jesus' sake. For God made his light shine in our hearts.' It is not just a matter of people being persuaded by convincing arguments. 'God made his light shine in our hearts to give us the light of the knowledge of the glory of God in the face of Christ' (2 Cor. 4:6).

This is what Paul earnestly desired to share with other people. He saw his task not as the presentation of his own ideas, theories and opinions, but as the proclamation of the once-crucified and now-risen Saviour. Yet he could also speak of his efforts to 'persuade' other people (2 Cor. 5:11). He used all of his very considerable powers of argument and persuasion to convince others of the truth of the gospel.

We have several times referred to C. S. Lewis's picture[6] of children playing burglars and then suddenly being pulled up. They aren't sure any longer whether this is just a game – was that a real footstep they heard? It is our hope that through this book someone may hear that footstep – not a footstep to be feared or dreaded, but one to be welcomed, for he comes not as a thief or robber but as the giver of life in all its fullness (John 10:10).

Notes

1.   *Understanding The Times* (Saint Andrew Press, Edinburgh, 1995), p.8.
2.   Quoted by D. Allen, in 'The End of the Modern World: a New Openness for Faith', *Princeton Seminary Bulletin*, n.s. XI, 1 (1990), p.12.
3.   F. Macdonald, *Prospects For Scotland* (National Bible Society of Scotland, Edinburgh, 1995), p.85.
4.   T. Gillespie in 'inSpire', Alumni Magazine of Princeton Theological Seminary, Summer 1998, p.2.
5.   The Press & Journal, 4 August 1998.
6.   C. S. Lewis, *Miracles* (Collins, London & Glasgow, 1947), p.98.

SUBJECT INDEX

believe it
or not!

Lack of evidence? Lack of interest? Lack of commitment? Just what is it that holds so many back from responding to the claims of Jesus Christ – especially when the Bible maintains that knowing him is the only way to know meaning, joy, and peace? Based on answers to a recent comprehensive survey, *Believe It Or Not!* analyses the main barriers to belief, and challenges those not yet convinced to think again about these vital issues.

'Hasn't science buried God? Aren't all religions the same? How can God allow evil to prosper? These questions are heard time and time again and they need clear answers. In this age when fewer and fewer people have ever been taught the message of the Bible, David Randall has carefully, ably and clearly given us a book that should help the honest enquirer understand the place of human life in the purposes of God.'

Howard Taylor, Chaplain to the University
Heriot-Watt, Edinburgh

'The greatest challenge facing the Church today is the communication of the Gospel to new generations. Such a task always begins with building bridges that enable engagement with the issues of faith. In this helpful book, David Randall uses straightforward logic and many illustrations to throw light on his arguments. I commend it to those who are seeking; and also to Christians prayerfully engaging with others.'

Douglas Nicol, General Secretary of the Board of National Mission
The Church of Scotland

Minister of Macduff Parish Church since 1971, David J. Randall is currently Vice Convener of the Church of Scotland's Board of National Mission, and a former Convener of its Apologetics Committee. He is married to Nan, and they have three sons, one daughter and one grandson. David enjoys reading and jogging, though not at the same time!

RUTHERFORD HOUSE
Encouraging Effective Ministry

17 Claremont Park,
Edinburgh, EH6 7PJ
www.rutherfordhouse.org.uk

ISBN 0-946068-82-8